KATJA PETROWSKAJA was born in [illegible] speaking family. She studied literat[illegible] then completed her PhD in Mosco[illegible] since 1999. She won the Ingeborg Bachmann Prize in 2013 and wrote her bestselling first book, *Maybe Esther*, in German. It was published in 2014 and was awarded the Schubart Literary Prize, the Ernst Toller Prize, the Aspekte Literature Prize and the Strega European Prize. It was a *Spiegel* bestseller and has been translated into nineteen languages.

'Perhaps Petrowskaja's ultimate achievement in this remarkable book is to have forged a language out of muteness; a language quiet enough to enable her to find a way to describe the indescribable events of the last century with more beauty and curiosity than horror' *Guardian*

'Unflinchingly potent … revolutionaries, war heroes, teachers and phantoms populate these magnetic pages'
Irish Independent

'There is a golden aspect to her prose, at times almost mystical, endlessly observing, recalling the Russian-Jewish artist Marc Chagall's series of "Lovers" paintings, his enraptured figures hovering just above the earth' *Financial Times*

'There's a literary miracle on every page here, the sort of book that makes you fall in love with reading. There's poetry and politics in this family memoir, but most of all there's the pleasure of being in the company of Petrowskaja's talent. A Proust for the Google age' PETER POMERANTSEV, author of *Nothing is True and Everything is Possible*

'This intimately told quest into the darkness of the twentieth century is luminously unforgettable. The rich humanism of Petrowskaja's gaze, her many-cultured, good-humoured sensitivity, and her visionary use of the themes that emerge from her family's histories – silence, muteness, disguise, survival – infuse this book with the qualities of a classic. *Maybe Esther*, on her civilising journey 'against time', will stay with me forever' KAPKA KASSABOVA, author of *Border*

'Rarely is research into family history this exciting, this moving. If this were a novel it would seem exaggerated and unbelievable. This is great literature' *Der Spiegel*

'Katja Petrowskaja's family now have a home: this book. She ties today with yesterday and draws it all together to be carried over into the future as the literature of tomorrow'
Frankfurter Rundschau

'Modern German literature is richer for this intelligent, flamboyant and extremely original voice' *Die Zeit*

MAYBE ESTHER

KATJA PETROWSKAJA

Translated from the German by Shelley Frisch

4th ESTATE • *London*

4th Estate
An imprint of HarperCollins*Publishers*
1 London Bridge Street
London SE1 9GF
www.4thEstate.co.uk

First published in Great Britain in 2018 by 4th Estate
First published in Germany as *Vielleicht Esther* by Suhrkamp Verlag Berlin in 2014

This 4th Estate paperback edition published in 2019

1

A catalogue record for this book is available from the British Library

ISBN 978-0-00-824531-3

CONTENTS

3: My Beautiful Poland / 77

4: In the World of Unstructured Matter / 121

MAYBE ESTHER

PROLOGUE

THANK GOOGLE

I would rather have set off from elsewhere than here, the wasteland around the train station that still attests to the devastation of this city, a city that was bombed and reduced to ruins in the course of victorious battles, as retribution, it seemed to me, seeing as how the war that had been the cause of immeasurable devastation, far and wide, had been steered from this very city, an endless blitzkrieg with iron wheels and iron wings. That is now so far in the past that this city has become one of the most peaceful cities in the world and pursues this peace almost aggressively, as if in remembrance of the war.

The train station was recently built in the middle of this city, and despite the much-touted peace the station was inhospitable, as though it embodied all the losses that no train could outrun, one of the most inhospitable places in our Europe, united every which way, yet still sharply bounded, a place that always feels drafty and where your gaze opens out onto a wasteland, unable to alight in an urban jungle, to rest on something before moving out of here, out of this void in the midst of the city, a void that no government can fill, no lavish buildings, no good intentions.

Again, it was drafty as I stood on the platform and my eyes once more swept across the huge letters

BOMBARDIER
Willkommen in Berlin

underneath the arc of the curved roof, noting the contours lackadaisically yet thrown as ever by the mercilessness of this welcome. It was drafty when an elderly gentleman came up to me and asked about this Bombardier.

Your thoughts go straight to bombs, he said, to artillery, to that terrible, unfathomable war, and why Berlin of all places should be welcoming us in that way, this lovely, peaceful, bombed-out city, which is aware of all that, it just can't be that Berlin bombards—so to speak—new arrivals like him with this word in huge letters, and what is meant by *welcome* anyway, who exactly is supposed to be bombarded, and with what. He was desperately seeking an explanation, he told me, because he was about to set off. I replied, somewhat astounded that my inner voice was addressing me in the form of an old man with dark eyes and an American accent, breathless and ever more agitated, almost wildly plying me with questions that I myself had played through a hundred times already, play it again, I thought, sinking deeper and deeper into these questions, into this distant realm of questions on the platform, and I replied that I, too, think of war right away, it's not a matter of age, I always think about the war as it is, especially here in this through station, which is not the final destination for anyone, never fear, you can keep on going, I thought, and that he was not the first who had wondered about that, to himself and to me. I am here too often, I thought for a second, maybe I'm a стрелочник, a shunter, the shunter is always the one to blame, but only in Russian, I thought, as the old man said, My name is Samuel, Sam.

And then I told him that *Bombardier* is a French musical now having a successful run in Berlin, many people come to the city to see it, can you imagine, all because of *Bombardier*, the Paris Commune or some such piece of history, nowadays two nights in a hotel plus musical all-inclusive, and that there already had been problems since, at this station, *Bombardier* is advertised only with this one word, without comment, it had even been in the newspaper, I said, I recall, that it claimed the word gave rise to false associations, there was even a court case that grew out of the city's dispute with the musical, linguists were called in, imagine that, to assess the potential of this word to incite violence, and the court delivered the verdict in favor of the freedom of advertising. I believed what I was saying more and more although I had no idea what this Bombardier on the arc of the central station meant and where it came from, but as I was speaking so enthusiastically and offhandedly and saying things I would certainly not define as a lie, my imagination took wing, and I drifted further and further without the slightest fear of going over the cliff, coiling and recoiling into the curves of this verdict that had never been pronounced, because those who don't lie can't fly.

Where are you traveling to? the old man asked me, and I told him everything without a second of hesitation, with the kind of verve I might use to excoriate some other musical, I talked about the Polish city my relatives had moved from a hundred years earlier, to Warsaw and then farther east, perhaps solely in order to bequeath to me the Russian language, which I was now so generously passing along to no one, *dead end* and *halt*, so I have to travel there, I said, to one of the oldest cities in Poland, where they, the forebears about whom nothing is known, had lived for two, three, or even four centuries, perhaps since the fifteenth century, when the Jews in this little Polish town had been granted privileges and become neighbors, the Others. And you? Sam asked, and I said I am Jewish, more by accident than design.

We're waiting for that train as well, Sam said after a brief pause, we, too, are taking the Warszawa Express. Taking this train, which looks like a thoroughbred horse as it looms up out of the fog, an express train that moves according to schedule but against time, into the zone of Bombardier, for us only, I thought, and the old man moved on to say that his wife was looking for the same thing, namely the world of her grandmother, who had come to the United States from a small White Russian village outside of Biała Podlaska, and yet it was neither his homeland nor his wife's, a hundred years have gone by and many generations, and none of them knew the language anymore either, but still, Biała Podlaska sounded to him like a forgotten lullaby, godknowswhy, a key to the heart, he said, and the village is called Janów Podlaski, and hardly anyone had lived there besides Jews and now only the others, and they were both going there to take a look at it, and, he really did keep saying *and* again and again, as though he was stumbling over an impediment, naturally nothing remained there, he said *naturally* and *nothing* in order to emphasize the senselessness of his journey, I, too, often say *naturally* or even *innately* as though this disappearance or this nothingness was natural or even self-evident. The landscape, however, the names of the places and a stud farm for Arabian horses that has been in existence since the early nineteenth century, established after the Napoleonic Wars and the top choice of the experts, everything was still there, they told me as though they had googled everything. A horse could cost a good million dollars there, Mick Jagger had already taken a look at horses from this stud farm at an auction, his drummer bought three, and now they would be going there, five kilometers from the Belarussian border, thank Google. There was even a horse cemetery there, no, the Jewish cemetery was not preserved, that was on the Internet as well.

I'm a Jew from Tehran, the old man said in English as we were still standing on the platform, Samuel is my new name. I came to New York from Tehran, Sam said. He knew Aramaic, had learned a good many things, and took his violin wherever he went. In the United States, he'd actually set out to study nuclear physics, but wound up applying to the conservatory, failed the entrance exam, and became a banker, but was no longer in that line of work either. Even after fifty years, his wife said when we were already sitting in the train and the metallic rainbow of "Willkommen in Berlin" was no longer weighing down on our heads, his wife said that whether he's playing Brahms, Vivaldi, or Bach, it all sounds Iranian. And he said it was fate that they had met me, I looked like the Iranian women of his childhood, he had wanted to say Iranian mothers, perhaps he even wanted to say *like my mother* but held back, and he added it was also a twist of fate that I was better versed in genealogy than they were, and that I was traveling to Poland with the same destination and the same train—assuming the urge to search for what has vanished can be defined as a destination at all, I replied. And no, it is not fate, I said, because Google watches over us like God, and when we search for something, it fleshes out our story, just like when you buy a printer on the Internet and you continue to be offered printers for a long time to come, and when you buy a backpack for school, you continue to get advertising for it for years, and let's not even mention online dating, and if you google yourself, at some point even your namesakes vanish, and what remains is *only you*, as though you have sprained your foot and limp, and suddenly the entire city limps, out of solidarity, perhaps, millions of limpers, they form a group, almost the majority. How is democracy supposed to work if you get only what you've already searched for and if you are what you search, and you never feel alone or you always do, since you never get the chance to meet the others, who are not like you, and that's how it is with the search, you come across like-minded people, God googles our paths, so that we stay put in our grooves, I always meet people who are looking for the same thing I am, I said, and that is why we, too, have met here, and the old man said, This is the very meaning of fate. He was obviously further along in exegesis than I.

All of a sudden I thought of the musical that had actually created a sensation here, when you saw the words *Les Misérables*, without comment, on the advertising spaces of the city, unlike the movie of the same name, which called the miserable ones *Prisoners of Fate*. The musical spoke to everyone with its *Les Misérables*, as though one needed constant consolation—Poor, miserable you!—or simply needed to have it pointed out that it is not merely one of us who is suffering, but indeed we all come together in suffering, because faced with these huge letters, faced with this wasteland in the middle of the city, all of us are miserable, not only the others, but I as well. And so the letters of Bombardier on the arc of the station roof fill us with their reverberation, the way organ music fills the church, and none can escape it.

And then I really did google it: Bombardier was one of the largest railway and airplane construction companies in the world, and this Bombardier, which sets our paths, had recently launched an ad campaign, "Bombardier YourCity." Quickly and safely. And now we were traveling from Berlin to Poland on the Warszawa Express, with the blessing of Bombardier, among curtains and napkins bearing the insignia WARS, an abbreviation as outmoded and bygone as Star Wars and other wars of the future.

CHAPTER I

AN EXEMPLARY STORY

Family Tree

A spruce is standing lonely.

—HEINRICH HEINE

As a child I thought a family tree was something like a Christmas tree, a tree with decorations from old boxes—some baubles break, fragile as they are, some angels are ugly and sturdy and remain intact through every move. In any case, a Christmas tree was the only family tree we had, bought new every year then thrown away, a day before my birthday.

I had thought that telling the story of the few people who happened to be my relatives was all that was needed to conjure up the entire twentieth century. Some of my family members were born to pursue their callings in life in the unswerving, implicit belief that they would fix the world. Others seemed to have come out of nowhere; they did not put down roots, they ran back and forth, barely touching the ground, and hung in the air like a question, like a skydiver caught in a tree. My family had just about everything, I had arrogantly thought, a farmer, many teachers, a provocateur, a physicist, and a poet—and plenty of legends.

We had

a revolutionary who joined the Bolsheviks and changed his name in the underground to one we have been using legally for close to a hundred years several workers in a shoe factory in Odessa, about whom nothing is known

a physicist who ran an experimental turbine factory in Kharkiv and vanished during the purges; his brother-in-law was told to turn against him in court because party loyalty was gauged by a person's willingness to sacrifice his own family members

a war hero named Gertrud, the husband of my aunt Lida, who was born when work was declared an end in itself, at first everyone worked a lot, then too much, and later still more, because exemplary achievements replaced norms and work became the meaning of life in the nation of proletarians and supermen, and so it came about that my future uncle was named Geroy Truda at birth, hero of labor, work hero, abbreviated to Gertrud

then there were Arnold, Ozjel, Zygmunt, Misha, Maria, Maybe Esther, maybe a second Esther and Madam Siskind, a deaf-mute student of Ozjel who sewed clothing for the entire city

many teachers who founded orphanages throughout Europe and taught deaf-mute children

Anna and Lyolya, who died in Babi Yar, and all the others there

a phantom named Judas Stern, my great-uncle

---

a peacock my grandparents bought for the deaf-mute children so they could enjoy its beauty

a Rosa and a Margarita, my floral grandmas

Margarita received a letter of recommendation for party membership in 1923, directly from Molotov, the future Soviet minister of foreign affairs, that's how we tell the story, as if it showed that we were always at the center of the action

my grandmother Rosa, who had the loveliest name of all speech therapists and waited for her husband longer than Penelope had

my grandfather Vasily, who went off to war and did not return to my grandmother Rosa for forty-one years. She never forgave him for his long odyssey, but—in our family there is always someone who says *but*—but, this someone said, they kissed, at the kiosk next to the subway station, when they were both over seventy, the Hotel Tourist was under construction just then, but Grandfather, my mother said, Grandfather wasn't able to leave the apartment anymore back then, and the Hotel Tourist wasn't built until later

my other grandfather, the revolutionary who had not only changed his name but also given his mother a new name in every Soviet questionnaire, depending on the way the political wind was blowing, his employment, and his taste in literature, until he came up with Anna Arkadyevna, that was Anna Karenina's name, who thus became my great-grandmother

---

We were happy, and everything within me resisted Leo Tolstoy's pronouncement that happy families are alike in their happiness and only the unhappy ones are unique, a pronouncement that lured us into a trap and brought out our penchant for unhappiness, as though only unhappiness was worth words, but happiness hollow.

Negative Numbers

My big brother taught me the negative numbers, he told me about black holes, as an introduction to a way of life. He conjured up a parallel universe where he was forever beyond reach, and I was left with the negative numbers. The only cousin I knew about was someone I rarely saw, even more rarely than her mother Lida, my mother's big sister. My strict uncle, my father's big brother, during his rare visits, gave me physics problems to solve on the topic of perpetual motion, as though constant motion could gloss over his absence in our lives. My two babushkas lived with us, but weren't all there: I was still a child when they reached the full incapacity of their advanced age. Other babushkas baked piroshki and cake, knitted warm sweaters and colorful caps, some even socks—socks, the aerobatics of knitting, *vysshiy pilotazh*, as people used to say. They brought the children to school and to music class, they picked them up, and in the summer they waited in their gardens for their grandchildren, in their dachas, little country huts. My babushkas lived with us on the seventh floor, and could not put down roots in the concrete. Both of them had floral names, and I secretly thought that the mallows that grew in front of our fourteen-floor building were connivers in Babushka Rosa and Babushka Margarita's plot to retreat into the plant kingdom.

They didn't have all their marbles, you might say, though in Russian you don't use the expression "all their marbles." Russians would ask, Don't you have them all at home? I was afraid of this question, although my babushkas were almost always at home, probably for my protection, even so, this not having them all at home, or even just the word "all," alarmed me, as though the others were privy to something about us that I wasn't, and knew who or what was actually missing.

Sometimes I thought I knew. Two of my grandparents were born in the nineteenth century, and it seemed to me that in the turmoil of the era one generation had been lost or skipped over, they truly were not *"at home"*; my friends' *great*-grandparents were younger than my grandparents, and it was left to me to foot the bill for two generations and face the music. I was the very youngest in a line of the youngest. I was the youngest there had ever been.

The feeling of loss worked its way, without warning, into my otherwise cheerful world, hovering over me, spreading its wings, depriving me of air and light, on account of a deficiency that may not have existed. Sometimes it struck like a bolt of lightning, a sudden swoon, throwing me off balance and leaving me gasping for breath, flailing about to regain my equilibrium, hit by a bullet that was never fired off, no one had said *hands up*!

These existential gymnastics in the struggle for balance struck me as a part of the family heritage, an innate reflex. In English class we practiced *hands up, to the sides, forward, down.*

I always figured that the word *gymnastics* came from the word *hymn*, as in *hymnastics*, in Russian both words start with a *g*, *gimnastika* and *gimn*, and I eagerly extended my hands upward in an attempt to touch the imperceptible sheath of the heavens.

There were many who had even fewer relatives than I. Some children had no brothers or sisters, no babushka or parents, and there were children who had sacrificed themselves for the homeland in the war, these children were brave heroes, they became our idols, they were always with us. We were not allowed to forget their names even at night, they had died many years before our birth, but back then we had no "back then," only a "now," in which war losses were said to constitute an inexhaustible supply of our own happiness, because the only reason we were alive, we were told, was that they had died for us, and we needed to be eternally grateful to them, for our peaceful normality and for absolutely everything. I grew up not in the cannibalistic but the vegetarian years, as Akhmatova dubbed them (and we all echoed her), and we attributed all losses to the war that was long since over, the war that bore no article or adjective, we simply said *war*; there aren't any articles in Russian anyway, and we did not specify which war, because we thought that there was only one, erroneously, since during our happy childhood our state was waging another war, down in the faraway south, for our safety, we were told, and for the freedom of others, a war that we were not allowed to acknowledge in spite of the daily losses, and I, too, did not acknowledge it until I was ten years old and saw the zinc casket in front of our apartment building, which contained the remains of a nineteen-year-old neighbor, a boy I could not recall even then, but I recall his mother to this day.

I had no reason to suffer. Yet I did suffer, from early on, although I was happy and loved, and surrounded by friends, embarrassed to be suffering, but suffering still with a loneliness that ranged from razor-sharp to bleakly bitter and I thought it stemmed only from a feeling of missing out on something. The luxurious dream of a big family at a long table followed me with the persistence of a ritual.

And yet our living room was full of my father's friends and my mother's adult students, dozens of students who always stood by her until in time, there were several generations of them at our table, and we took the same photographs as other families: against the backdrop of the dark floral curtains lots of merry, slightly overexposed faces, all turned toward the camera, at a long, beautifully decorated table. I don't know exactly when I first picked up on the hints of discord during my family's loud, exuberant festivities.

You could count the list of those who could be considered part of my family on the fingers of two hands. I had no need to practice the piano scale of aunt, uncle, cousin, first cousin once removed and her husband, cousin, and great-uncle—up and down, up and down, and I was terrified of that piano, that aggressive totality of the keyboard.

In an earlier time, before we had our big dinner parties, a large family was a curse, because relatives could be members of the White Army, saboteurs, noblemen, kulaks, overeducated *"enemies of the people"* living abroad, their children, and other dubious characters, and everyone was under suspicion, so families suffered a convenient loss of memory, often in order to save themselves, even though it rarely helped, and on special occasions, any relatives who might fit these categories were generally forgotten, often hidden from the children, and families dwindled; whole branches of the family were erased from memory, extended families were pared down until there was nothing left of them but the joke about the two men with the same last name who are asked if they're related. Certainly not, they reply: we don't even have the same last name!

The List

One day, the relatives from deep in my past were suddenly standing in front of me, murmuring their merry messages in familiar-sounding languages. Well then, I thought, I'll have them make the family tree blossom, fill in the gaps, and mend the feeling of loss, but they crowded together in front of me without faces or histories, like fireflies of the past that shed light on small spaces around them, maybe a couple of streets or incidents, but not on themselves.

I knew their names. All these Levis—the name of my great-grandmother, her parents, and her siblings—would be scattered around the world if they were still alive. I knew that there were Gellers or Hellers; no one knows exactly which. I knew about a Simon Geller only from a note in Russian, a translation from a Hebrew newspaper that is no longer available anywhere. I knew the last Krzewins, the descendants of the Hellers, the relatives with the name that crunches like snow under your feet, like *kovrizhka*, gingerbread, between your teeth. There were also the Sterns, which was my grandfather's name until he was twenty. My name would be Stern as well if the Russian Revolution hadn't triumphed, and that was the name of his many brothers and sisters, his parents, and their many brothers and sisters, and his grandparents with their entire clan, if there were truly as many of them as I liked to imagine.

My distant relatives, Krzewins and Levis, had lived in Łódź, Kraków, Kalisz, Koło, Vienna, Warsaw, Kiev, and Paris, up to 1940, as I realized only recently, and in Lyon, my mother told me. Ruzija attended the university in Vienna, and Juzek studied in Paris, I recall my grandmother saying. I never learned who Ruzija and Juzek were; they were simply relatives of mine. Maybe it was the other way around: Ruzija studied in Paris and Juzek in Vienna. The word *conservatory* came up, but I don't recall to whom it applied. And I recall being told that Ruzija and Juzek had to clean the sidewalk with a toothbrush. In Łódź, Kalisz, Warsaw, it was perhaps still vacation time, and at the conservatory the semester had not yet begun; they were at home and not in Paris or Vienna. When I heard this as a child, I thought their location was Switzerland, because our newspapers were reporting that in Switzerland everything was squeaky clean, and some people made a habit of squatting with little brushes and shampoo in front of their houses and scrubbing the sidewalk. I pictured the country drowning in soap bubbles, this country—or another—in its gleaming, unattainable spotlessness.

Some of my relatives' names were so common that it made

no sense to look for them. It would have been a search for people who happened to bear the same name, because in the lists they all appear together, next to one another like neighbors, intermingled, and mine cannot be distinguished from hundreds of others with the very same names, and anyway it would not have been possible for me to distinguish my family from strangers the way you separate wheat from chaff, seeing as it would have been a *selection*, and I didn't want that, not even the word. The more of the same name there were, the less likely was the chance of finding my relatives among them, and the less likely this chance was, the clearer it became to me that I had to consider each person on the lists one of my own.

I painstakingly compiled their names, tracking down every Levi, Krzewin, Geller or Heller, and at some point, when I was standing in Warsaw's military church facing the long lists that ran from wall to wall in tiny print, lists with the names of the dead from the Katyń massacre—why do we automatically look for our own names even in the lists of the dead?—I found Stanisław Geller on the lists and, in the chapel of the Katyń military church, I declared my affinity with all namesakes, including Stanisław, as though he and everyone I had yet to find also belonged to my family, all the Gellers and Hellers, and all the Krzewins and Sterns. Every Stern seemed like a secret relative, even those as remote as stars in the sky.

Years earlier, when I was in New York, I leafed through the yellow pages, the yellowed pages of an old phone book. Where are my grandfather's brothers and sisters? Where are his father's brothers and sisters, whose name was Stern and who had disappeared from Odessa in every direction? Were their descendants singing with the Velvet Underground? Did they have a bank? Were they teaching in Massachusetts, at MIT, or were they still working in a shoe factory? After all, somebody's got to be working.

There were many Sterns in the phone book. Eight whole pages. Yellow-star Sterns in the yellowed phone book. Should I call up each one of them and ask? What did you do before 1917? Are you still waiting for the poor relatives from the east? Even after a hundred years? And the luminaries, should I include them on my list, or should they include me on theirs?

Who told me that one of our Levis was a bookkeeper in a button factory in Warsaw? Another Levi made the 501 jeans, the best ones I knew back when I began my search. He surely wasn't one of us; I can't imagine that someone in my family could have a yen for profit or any idea of how to seize opportunities that came along. As my thoughts continued to turn to the button factory in Warsaw or elsewhere, my conviction grew that no one who had remained in Poland could have made it onto a list like that.

I recalled a rescue list I'd seen in a movie, and I went through it as though it were possible that someone from my family could be recorded there and thus rescued, showing up on the Internet. I read one name after the other as though in search of winning numbers, as though I would have recognized someone.

There was no Levi or Krzewin, but I did find an Itzhak Stern, also a bookkeeper, though in a factory in Kraków. He was not a relative of mine, because my Sterns were in Odessa, and those who hadn't emigrated much earlier were making revolution in the underground, yet one war later there were no rescue missions for them in Odessa and no more lists. Should I put this Stern onto my list anyway, because the others can't be tracked down? Or would that be attempted theft?

There are, as is well known, games without winners.

Hello, my name is Joe, and I work in a button factory.

One day my boss came up to me and asked if I was busy.

I said no.

So he said:

Then push this button with your right hand.

Hello, my name is Joe . . .

The Recipe

The revelation that people left us struck me unawares; it settled over me like a shadow, covering my head like the basin that Don Quixote had used as a helmet and in which, centuries later, my blind babushka cooked plum preserves. Now the basin had been gathering dust on top of the cupboard for years.

When Lida, my mother's older sister, passed away, I came to understand the meaning of the word *history*. My longing was fully developed, I was ready to submit myself to the windmills of memory, and then she died. I was standing there with bated breath, ready to ask, rooted to the spot, and if this had been a comic book, my speech bubble would have been empty. History begins when there are no more people to ask, only sources. I had no one left to question, no one who could still recall these times. All I had were fragments of memory, notes of dubious value, and documents in distant archives. Instead of asking questions at the right time, I had choked on the word *history*. Had Lida's death brought me to adulthood? I was at the mercy of history.

The only thing I have from Aunt Lida is a recipe for a refreshing drink known as kvass. The recipe recently jumped out at me from a pile of unpaid bills, as though I owed something to Lida. After the war, Aunt Lidiya, or Lida, as we called her, was known as the classical beauty of the Kiev Pedagogical Institute, Lida from the Department of Defectology, as orthopedagogy is still called back home. Yet when I knew Lida, the same Lida who peered down at us serenely and unflappably from photographs, she was a shuffling creature in an apron who had said nothing for years, just served, one course after another, then into the kitchen and back again, on plates with a gilded rim. Eat! She had been the last one in the family to teach the deaf-mute children, she knew the secret, she knew patience, she cooked in silence, and now she was gone.

For a long time I couldn't figure out what the EBP.KBAC at the very top of the slip of paper might signify. I stared at this EBP, thinking that the Cyrillic abbreviation could be understood as EBPопейский, YEVropeysky, European, or just as easily as EBPейский, JEWreysky, Jewish kvass—an innocent utopia of the Russian language and the *Urbi et Orbi* of my aunt, as though Europe and the Jews were descended from one root, and this recipe and this abbreviation fostered the refreshing hypothesis that all Jews, even those who were no longer Jews at all anymore, were among the last Europeans, having, after all, read everything that constitutes Europe. Or didn't my aunt want to write out the word *Jewish*, because the incomplete and abbreviated form left open yet another interpretive option, for example, that this drink was not all that Jewish, but only allusively, only a little, in spite of the garlic?

The recipe turned out to be a kind of encrypted poetic exercise. I had never picked up on anything Jewish about my aunt, and there was nothing there anyway, aside from her penchant for cooking these dishes, which I couldn't figure out until after her death, and I understood that she of all people, who wanted nothing to do with the whole pain of saying "Jew" and thinking of graves right away and who, because she was still alive, could not be a Jew, had learned a tasty, juicy set of recipes from her grandparents, who were still Jewish, and had adopted many things that even her mother didn't know. Now gefilte fish, strudel, and chopped herring were part of Lida's Ukrainian cooking repertoire.

INGREDIENTS:

One large bunch of lettuce
One large garlic bulb
One large bunch of dill

[One line is missing here]

You boil water and let it cool down to room temperature.
You rinse the lettuce, then you cut off the root and stem, then you cut everything into small pieces and peel the garlic.

This epistle was addressed to me. Who writes recipes in direct speech with a hint of pathos?

You should rinse and cut the dill
Then you stir everything and put it into a three-liter jar.

Had Lida been addressing me with this *you*, or people in general?

The three-liter jar, *tryokhlitrovaya banka*, rattled me even more. A generation of utensils lies between the kitchen over there, with its three-liter jar to store brine, its cheesecloth to strain the broth, its cast-iron pan, and my kitchen here. Where can you buy cheesecloth in Berlin? Over there we have little rags and worn-out towels and cheesecloth, copper basins and wooden spoons for the plum preserves, all of which had once been bought, and if you asked when, you were told, after the war.

She kept everything to herself, and when she died, all her strudels, gefilte fish, and sweet sausages with raisins went with her, her cookies, the ones with dried plums, the ones with honey, lemons, and nuts, and she also took the word *tzimmes* with her, as though everything had to remain a mystery. She kept everything to herself, her beauty as a young woman, all the reading she'd done, she kept it all inside, just for her husband, a war hero, felled by seven shots, one of the handsomest heroes, she said nothing about her illnesses and worries, her teaching methods, her increasing deafness, when she went in and out of the kitchen, she said nothing about the birthdays of the dead, the birthdays of the murdered, which she commemorated for years, alone, she also said nothing about other dates, she remembered everyone and everything that touched her in life, she said nothing about the war and the before and the after and all the trains and all the cities, the grief about her father, who survived the war, but did not return to the family and later lived next door, for years, in one of the nine-floor prefabricated buildings of our anonymous Soviet development. As she grew older and then old, she was still waiting, and eventually she turned mute, because she understood that she was going deaf, and so she returned to the deaf-mute children she had taught all her life, and if she could have, she would have kept her death to herself as well. I hadn't asked her about anything and now wonder why I missed out on her so completely, her and her life, as though I had accepted her resolute deaf-muteness right from the start, her service and her role. What was I up to back then, anyway, when she could have given me everything, the recipe for ЕВР.КВАС, for example, to me and all of Европа?

Perpetual Motion

Abstract thinking is not my forte, Uncle Vil, my father's older brother, liked to quip, when I talked about friction losses. To test me, he gave me the most ingenious problems to solve when he visited, problems about Egyptian triangles, the model of perpetual motion, as though a fundamental truth would be revealed to me if I found solutions to Vil's problems. But I never did.

He himself was the product of a Soviet metempsychosis, a transmutation of the energies between state, soul, and machine, the perpetual motion of my country. Vil was born in 1924, eight months after Lenin's death, when the country was expressing its grief by naming factories, cities, and villages after him. Lenin lived, his name made power plant turbines revolve, *your name shall be Lenin*, and the lightbulbs glow. Hence my grandparents named their firstborn Vil, after the late Vladimir Ilyich Lenin, who was considered the grandfather of all Soviet children, so Lenin had grandchildren, albeit no children. Even fifty years later, we were his grandchildren, and we said Dedushka Lenin, Grandpa Lenin, because everything was in motion but time.

There were all kinds of marvelous creatures, such as Rabfak, Oblmortrest, Komsomol, Molokokoopsoyuz; everything was abbreviated and compounded back then, Mosselprom, Narkompros, or Cheka, the most long-lived organization, which later turned into GPU, NKVD, KGB, FSB. I knew a Ninel, a name formed by spelling Lenin backward; a Rem, a son of Trotskyites, from Revolutsiya Mirovaya—World Revolution; a Roi, from Revolution October International; and I even knew a very nice Stalina.

Maybe the choice of name also had to do with the fact that my grandparents could still speak Yiddish: the Yiddish force of will—*vil*—shone through, and, in fact, no one in our family was as single-mindedly determined as Vil, who never stopped optimizing his efficiency, and even the authorities went along with him. In 1940, when he applied for a passport in Kiev at the age of sixteen, he got a document with a statement on the fifth line that he was Russian even though his parents were Jewish and had the corresponding note in their passports. With his blond mop of hair, blue eyes, broad shoulders, and narrow hips, Vil looked like the valiant Ivan from the fairy tale. It remains a mystery what mathematical operation could have led a Jewish couple to produce a Russian child, not even at birth, but at a passport agency. As a result, Vilya, as we called him, became a full-fledged Russian and shed the weight of his Jewish background, which receded to a mere detail, a superfluous add-on that was better left unmentioned. Besides, there was no cause to look back; there was only the future, for the world is vast, and knowledge infinite.

Vil's little brother, my father Miron, born eight years later, carried on his grandfather's name, Meir, in a modified form, and had the word *Jew* in his passport. However, for him there was no more Jewishness, so Miron also became a Russian, citizen of a nation of readers. He looked back at his ancestry pensively and with respect, if also a bit bewildered as to what he had to do with it.

The entire Soviet Union was against the force of gravity and dreamed of flying; Vil wanted to build airplanes. Even his body was aerodynamic, small and agile enough to go through life without friction losses. Vil could have stepped right out of the Soviet air force hymn everyone sang back then: *We were born to make fairy tales real, to overcome space and expanse, we received steel arm-wings from Reason, our heart is an engine in flames*. My heart beat faster and higher when I heard this hymn, fifty years later, especially the rising melody, *Ever higher and higher and higher the flight of our metal birds steers, each of our propellers respires the tranquility of our frontiers.*

At the age of eighteen Vil went to the front, like his entire class. They were packed into uniforms and sent off without the slightest notion of war, only of heroism. No sooner were they on the front in Mozdok in the Caucasus than the recruits charged into an antitank ditch under crossfire. When they had filled the ditch with their bodies, the tanks rolled over them. Vilya never told his parents exactly what had happened there at Mozdok; the only one to know was his brother Miron, who was eleven at the time. Miron retained this knowledge forever, maybe on behalf of his brother.

When the ditch was searched for survivors, Vil was found way at the bottom, squashed and shot through the groin. A miracle that there had even been a search, my father said.

Vil had severe contusions and traumatic epilepsy, and spent months in hospitals. He found his family in Ashgabat, thousands of miles from the Caucasus. Now a disabled war veteran, he was not beaten down by his injuries; instead, he used them as a motivating force and at the tender age of nineteen became the chairman of the Sports and Conscription Committee of Turkmenistan, the youngest minister in the Soviet Union.

He interrupted his university studies several times when epileptic seizures resulted in weeks of exhaustion. His tongue had to be held to prevent choking; my father kept talking about this tongue he had to hold, and every time he was surprised at his own words. How could Vilya still believe in Soviet power after the antitank ditch? I asked my father, and my father said that no one with doubts survived.

Eventually Vil studied mechanics and mathematics in Leningrad, exchanged air for water, and became a specialist in hydroacoustics. He had to solve the same problems as he had faced with flight, but resistance is stronger in water. Vilya optimized submarines so that the crew could hear everything without being heard, friction was avoided, and secrets kept.

He worked, worked, and worked on his own joyful wisdom, exploring the sound field and its inherent processes and the hydrodynamic problems of turbulence noise and the nonstationary functions of hydroacoustics. He even applied his sense of humor to his dialectical thinking, to his perpetuum mobile. In the name of our peace he worked for the war, but he himself spoke of maintaining equilibrium between forces, as though this was also just a question of mechanics.

Like Vil, I was born as a part of the state's metabolic cycle, a hundred years after Lenin. I celebrated my birthdays together with Lenin, minus a hundred. I knew this would always help me to find my coordinates in the history of the world, but the vitality of the up-and-coming young state that was given to my uncle by birth had long since withered away. When I seemed doomed not to come up with solutions to his perpetuum mobile problems, I sensed how alien we were to each other. My uncle knew that I would never solve the problems he posed. If a solution were to be found for the perpetuum mobile, all disparities would be eliminated, as would questions of proximity, warmth, doubt, and possibly even kinship, because in Vil's problems, everything human was regarded as a friction loss, as an obstacle to the incessant motion of hidden energies, my uncle's dream. Maybe Vilya wasn't joking at all—*Abstract thinking isn't your forte!*—when he left the research field of friction losses to me, in his stead.

Neighbors

I spent a large part of my childhood in Kiev in a new fourteen-floor apartment house on the left bank of the Dnieper, in a neighborhood that developed after the war and seemed to have no past, only a tidy future. But *"no one is forgotten and nothing is forgotten,"* as the poet Olga Bergholz wrote in remembrance of the one million casualties of the Siege of Leningrad. This line was borne in the heart, and replaced memory throughout the land. There was no escaping it since it assumed the role of prophecy, with its revealed truth and concealed lies; we were called on to forget no one and nothing in order that we forget who or what was forgotten. Our backyard games extended beyond jump rope and dodge ball to endless rounds of a cops-and-robbers-like game of "us" against "the fascists," thirty-five years after the war.

My street was named Ulitsa Florentsii, in honor of our beautiful Italian sister city. We were fortunate to live there because our address conveyed the beauty of Italy and our connection to the world of beauty, meaning that we too could be beautiful, that we too were raised in the spirit of the Renaissance to experience a rebirth and be situated in the center of the universe, albeit behind the Iron Curtain. The ceremonial opening of Ulitsa Florentsii took place in 1975, and a plaque was attached to our building. The building belonged to a Soviet ministry, so we called it Sovmin House, and in comparison with the nine-story prefabricated buildings in the Soviet barracks style that surrounded our courtyard, our Sovmin house was a luxury in brick. However, no ministers actually lived here; the residents were civil servants of the state apparatus, middle managers, low-ranking supervisors, teachers with well-worn book collections, cleaning ladies, cooks, secretaries, electricians, engineers. We never found out what we had done to merit an apartment in this socialist paradise—four rooms with built-in closets, an alcove for the refrigerator, two loggias, and attic space. In the first weeks after we moved in, my father met in the elevator a KGB case officer who had interrogated him ten years earlier, and he came home with a variant of "*My home is my castle.*" My home is *their* castle, he said.

Later on, the families of the American consulate staff moved in, and once, on July 4, they ran up a big American flag on their balconies, as though they had conquered our castle. In 1977, when the flamboyant and boisterous Florence soccer team came to Kiev, our street had a second ceremonial opening, although we had been living there for a long time. The Italians were surprised to discover us in our Kievan Florence, as though we were Native Americans being discovered by Europeans. What a piece of news that people live here! The plaque was taken down from one side of our building and attached to the other.

The building was full of women who had moved from villages to the city in their youth. As they grew older, they began to forget their hastily learned and never fully rooted Russian and sank back into the embraces of their warm Ukrainian. When they retired, they pulled out their floral headscarves, with the knot facing forward, and looked so rustic that it was hard to imagine that they'd ever taken them off. They gathered downstairs on the bench in front of the fourteen-floor colossus, shelled sunflower seeds, and exchanged the latest gossip. One of the few elderly men who lived in our building—the men died decades before the women—sat on the balcony somewhere quite high up and played folk songs on the accordion that resounded mournfully across our monumental courtyard and accompanied us as we went our various ways.

I knew very few of the neighbors, and even they were just passing acquaintances. One couple, a charming woman and her husband, a military doctor, always moved with grace and dignity. We did not know quite what to make of their daughter, and we never approached her; we knew nothing back then about Down syndrome. In those days, no one kept such a child at home—maybe it was even prohibited—but the other residents, held back by timidity and admiration of the family, never indulged in idle gossip. My mother told me that the beautiful woman was an orphan from the Spanish Civil War who had been brought to the allied Soviet Union in the late 1930s.

I got to know two other neighbors, both of whom were born during the war year of 1941: Sergey, a war orphan from

Ossetia, and Vadim, who was raised by partisans in Polesie. In the other wing lived Boris, a talkative man of an indeterminate age, always cheerful and forthcoming, the only one who had crawled out of the mass grave in a small Jewish town in 1941 when all other residents, from young to old, were murdered. Only much later did I find out that the uncanny monster that we girls in the courtyard between the long rows of high-rises had always feared—we called him The Madman—was the son of the fragile Boris, and maybe the final offspring of the vanished Jewish town.

Sometimes letters were addressed to us at Venice Street, Ulitsa Venetsii. Our building was situated on a canal, which not all letter writers knew. The letters arrived, because there was no Ulitsa Venetsii in Kiev, and so we were responsible for all of Italy. Because of this Venice, water came pouring into my dreams and flooded everything in them, but rescue always arrived when the water had risen as far as my seventh floor, always in the form of a golden gondola from a misty distance that came for me alone. I gave no thought to the neighbors drowning below me, forgetting them in my dreams.

Three floors below us there lived the lonely Makarovna, an elderly Ukrainian villager who had survived collectivization as a child only to lose her parents and fiancé in the war. For years she sat on the bench in front of our building in slippers and a headscarf. She was the feistiest of all, the brashest and unhappiest, always tipsy, sometimes amusing but never cheerful, and she gave us children candy so old it seemed to have dated back to the war provisions of last resort. In her bright yellow headscarf with shiny flowers in maroon and green, in her dark blue dressing gown—the retired woman's uniform—and a look of intensity in her faintly bulging eyes, she struck me as one of the last of the strong, wild, beautiful people that had once settled here at the threshold of the Ukrainian steppe. Later she gave me all kinds of superfluous things, felt boots for infants or thickly embroidered handkerchiefs, which I have kept to this day; she gave things away because she needed money, but I didn't understand that back then. From time to time she recounted jumbled bits and pieces about the war, family members who had died, and the collective farms known as kolkhozy, but either I hadn't been paying enough attention or her delirium was making her mix up the Soviet catastrophes; in any case the years did not match up. In some accounts her family died in the war, but in others the family starved on the kolkhoz, and her fiancé had never come back, or had never existed, as I secretly feared. The war was to blame, that was the only part that was certain.

In the Museum

I wanted to go back up and look at the bicorne that Napoleon lost at Waterloo, but my daughter dragged me down to the ground floor for the twentieth century. I sought to distract her with Dürer and Luther, but in vain; she brought me to the 1920s, where we raced through the strikes, the hunger, and Berlin's golden age, for she wanted to go on, to go *there*, and as we neared the 1930s, I tensed up. She pulled me along to join up with a tour for adults; Let's not, I said, but she reassured me, I know the score, Mama, and her comfort with the subject discomfited me more than her knowledge. She was eleven. We strode through the seizure of power, the ban on forming associations, the persecution of Communists, and when we were standing in front of the chart with the Nuremberg Laws and the tour guide—the *Führerin*, funny that's the word for the woman doing this job, she was just in the middle of talking about the Führer—launched into an explanation of who, and what percent, my daughter asked me in a loud whisper, Where are we here? Where are we on this chart, Mama? The question really ought to be asked not in the present tense but in the past, and the subjunctive: where would we have been if we had lived then, if we had lived in this country—if we had been Jewish and had lived here back then. I know this lack of respect for grammar, and I, too, ask myself questions of this sort, where am I on this picture, questions that shift me from the realm of imagination into reality, because avoidance of the subjunctive turns imagination into recognition or even statement, you take another's place, catapult yourself there, into this chart, for example, and thus I try out every role on myself as though there was no past without an *if*, *as though*, or *in that case*.

Where are we on this chart, Mama? my daughter asked. I was frightened by her directness, and to protect her from being frightened, I hastened to reassure her that we were not on it at all, we would have been in Kiev by that point or already evacuated, and by the way we weren't even born yet, this chart has nothing to do with us, and now I had almost said *if*, *but*, and *as though* after all, when a man from the guided group turned to me and said, By the way, *we* have paid.

Even before I understood that he was telling me that the guided tour was not free of charge and that he thought that I too should pay or we would be freeloaders, my daughter and I, as though we had filched this eight-euro history, although, thanks anyway, I would not filch this kind of thing, so before I understood that without paying we had no right to stand in front of the chart or on it, that we had come to the paying circle too late; even before or as I thought all of that, tears came to my eyes, although I wasn't crying at all, something was crying in me, I was cried for, and also the man was cried for within me, although he had no need of it, because he was in the right, we hadn't paid, or rather, we actually had, but there is always someone who hasn't.

CHAPTER 2

ROSA AND THE MUTE CHILDREN

Shimon the Hearer

He who does not find himself
finds that his family will swallow him whole.
—ANCIENT CHINESE PROVERB

Seven generations, said my mother, two hundred years long we have taught deaf-mute children how to speak; my mother always said "we," although she herself never taught deaf-mute children, she taught history. Surely she couldn't think that teaching deaf-mutes and teaching history were one and the same profession. The way she described it, we would forever remain captive in this selfless dedication, and even future generations would not be free of the responsibility of the We, the responsibility of teaching others, of living for others, especially for their children. These seven generations sound like the stuff of a fairy tale, as though seven generations were enough to reach eternity, to attain the word.

We have always taught, my mother said, we have all been teachers, and there is no other path for us. She said it with such conviction that it sounded like one of those adages that our country thought tried and true, like "A voice cries in the desert," or "A prophet is without honor in his own country."

Her sister, her mother, her grandfather, and all her grandfather's brothers and sisters, his father, and his father's father taught deaf-mute children; they founded schools and orphanages and lived under one roof with these children, they shared everything with them. These altruists drew no distinction between their job and their life. My mother loved the word *altruist*; they were all altruists, she said, and she was sure that she, too, carried this altruistic heritage within her, but I was equally certain that I did not.

When my mother told me how our ancestors spread out across Europe and founded schools for deaf-mutes in Austria-Hungary, in France and Poland, I recalled the passage in the Old Testament, or so I thought, but it was actually in the New Testament: Abraham begat Isaac. Isaac begat Jacob. Jacob begat Judah and his brothers. Judah begat Perez and Zerah with Tamar—and more unfamiliar names. I knew this passage as vaguely as my own genealogy, but it seemed to me that our set of ancestors had no end either. One generation after the other, beyond our line of vision and beyond the horizon of family memory, taught speaking to the deaf-mutes. Do you hear their fervid whispering?

> *Sh'ma Yisrael, in the morning and the evening, Sh'ma Yisrael, Hear, O Israel, hear me!*

The first ancestor we knew by name was Shimon Heller, Simon Geller in Russian. Maybe he was following the call of his Hebrew name; *Shimon* means "he has heard, the one who has heard from God and is heard by him." The first disciple who heeded and followed Jesus was named Simon, I thought, although this story had no meaning for my Jewish relatives. My Shimon founded a school for deaf-mute children in Vienna, during the first half of the nineteenth century. He taught children how to speak so that they would be heard;

otherwise his brothers in the faith would regard them as mentally ill, because the faculties of understanding and reason, they thought back then, reside in spoken language. To be heard is to belong.

Sound by sound, word by word, day by day, they learned to pray. I had grown up in the family of the Soviet Union sister nations; all were alike, and all had to learn my native tongue, but none had to learn prayers. All belonged to our We. I proudly believed that my ancestors taught the orphans of all nations. For an unacceptably long period of time, I couldn't imagine what language my relatives spoke back then, what language they taught the children. My cosmopolitan present made me think they had taught the deaf-mute children to speak in all the languages of the world, as though deaf-muteness and orphanhood made for a blank page and the freedom to adopt any language and any history. As I saw it, our Jewishness was deaf-mute, and deaf-muteness was Jewish. This was my history and my heritage, yet it was not me.

Sh'ma Yisrael, hear me Israel, where is Israel?

I sifted through stacks of documents, looking for evidence of us in the old papers and on the Internet. The search command highlighted the word *deaf* in yellow, as though Google knew that yellow was the color of Jewishness, just as I knew that Google highlighted any searched term in bright yellow. Every story with the yellow *deaf* became a building block of my past, of my Internet Jewishness. Maybe my people had stepped right out of the Talmud, out of the story of the two deaf-mutes who lived near the rabbi and always followed him into the school where he taught, and sat next to him, observing him attentively and moving their lips along with him. The rabbi prayed for them, and at some point it became apparent that they knew everything the rabbi had taught his students; they had learned everything with their eyes. I tried to follow up on all the other stories with the yellow *deaf*, reading the passages surrounding the yellow highlightings and expecting these deaf stories to flutter up and take on a life of their own.

At the beginning of the history of my family stood a translation. In 1864, the writer and proponent of Jewish Enlightenment Faivel Goldschmidt wrote an article about Simon Geller and his school in a Lemberg-issued Hebrew newspaper, full of enthusiasm about Simon's personality and his work. Sixty years later, the text was translated into Russian by Simon's grandson, Ozjel Krzewin, and another sixty years after that, my mother discovered Ozjel's translation in an archive in Kiev, together with other documents about my relatives' schools. However, the Hebrew newspaper with Goldschmidt's article was no longer traceable. Our family's heritage is predicated on a questionable translation without a source text, and I am now telling the story of this family in German without there ever having been a Russian original.

My mother said, Always with the pencil, they all learned with the pencil, the point in the mouth of the teacher, the end in the mouth of the child. That wasn't in Goldschmidt's article, but my mother knew it. She told me about the pencil, amused by the simple trick, yet somewhat put off by how close the mouths came to each other. The pencil vibrated, and the children noticed how the language originates out of the tongue.

"For every illness, even the most severe, the Lord God sends healing," Ozjel Krzewin translated the article about his grandfather, as though the latter had been a Jewish holy man. After two years the children could read and write Hebrew and German, and they could read lips fluently. After five years, the article went on to say, Geller's pupils could speak so clearly that their speech barely differed from those who had been endowed with hearing. They set their heavy tongues in motion and lifted off their vocal burdens. Their prophet Moses had also had an unwieldy mouth and a heavy tongue.

When Shimon was still in Vienna, an adult came into his school. The man's father had died, but he could not pray, because he was deaf-mute. He wanted to learn to pray in spoken language, and when he was able to, he went to the cemetery to the grave of his father, who had died many years earlier, to say kaddish. Even newspapers reported on this.

Ozjel appended his own name, Krzewin, to the name Geller in the translation. Did he want to highlight the relationship, or was the word already in the original text, an added name that Simon had earned? One Polish friend tells me that people named Krzewin are disseminators of knowledge; another says that *krzew* means "bush": maybe your Krzewins planted trees. But the Jews had no land, I thought, they planted their trees in the air. I liked the idea that even the name of my ancestors was evidence of this exuberant urge to learn. I leafed through *The History of Judaism*, six volumes, *The History of the Eastern European Jewry*, two volumes, *The History of the Jews*, one volume. I walked back and forth at the Judaica shelves of the library.

I did not find a Simon Geller in the many thick books about Vienna and its institutions for the deaf and mute. The definitive text on the subject, *The General Austrian Israelite Deaf-Mute Institute in Vienna, 1844–1926*, had a Simon Heller for the time period of our Heller or Geller, but he was the director of an institute for the blind. That has to be him, said the lady in the archive; in the small world of pedagogy for disabled students there can only have been one Simon Heller.

The school started in Vienna, then made its way through rural Polish areas, through Galicia, like a traveling circus, staying briefly in a city, a town, a shtetl, before Simon moved on with his family, the orphans, and the children who were sent by their parents.

I peered inside and listened, thinking of the many selfless men of the Jewish Enlightenment who were inspired by the idea that to spread learning is to pass it from mouth to mouth. For these people, who were obsessed with hearing, the spoken language was everything. I gesticulated, called out, opened my lips, I tried saying *Sh'ma Yisrael,* again and again, *Sh'ma Yisrael*, as though I had never spoken, I shook the air, *Sh'ma Yisrael*, I wanted so much to be heard, putting my tongue and my language to the test, I tried to tell the stories, to render them in my foreign German, I told the stories, one after the other, but I did not myself hear what I was saying.

A Flight

When Shimon, the teacher, returned from a fund-raising trip and strode along the town's weather-beaten buildings, I did not let him out of my sight. God lived in these side streets: Poland, Polyń, Polonia, Polania, *po-lan-ya*, here-lives-God, three Hebrew words that made a Promised Land for the Jews out of the Slavic Poland, and they all lived here, driven by language. I did not let him out of my sight while he was running through the narrow streets to his children, and then, behind the next corner, he took off from the earth and flew through the starlit sky over the little town. Why not fly, what with all the worries in the world, fly, besotted and wistful, so many children, one's own and the orphans, like stars in the sky, like six hundred thirteen commandments, you can't count higher than that on one walk, I've tried to, they fly toward tomorrow, parallel to time and space, sometimes crosswise, following their own trajectory and the wise and stern books that we will never read and understand, the paths in the towns shimmer, dark green, my evening stroll, my hunt for Shimon, the teacher, who stuffs small, colorful glass balls from Vienna into the pockets of his black overcoat, which is darker than the night, sucking candy from Lemberg, a tad tart, because a tongue needs to carry a tang, and he always has a pencil with him, a *kościół*, a church, a jug, a candlestick, chase after him, a whirlwind in the sky full of flying objects, another church with bulbous copper spires and a sloping golden cross, then a fiddle and blue flower of a boy with big, long-lashed eyes, taking a few more turns over the earth of their beloved Polania, their Promised Land of Polonia, the house of God, and it is here that the story of a family, of kin, can begin, and maybe even this story.

The Gate

My first trip abroad, in the summer of 1989, took me to Poland. The country was aquiver with shock therapy, the term attached to the economic experiment that lifted price controls. We had only six days, one of them for Oświęcim. I remember looking out the window at the flat countryside, which seemed familiar, as though I hadn't gone away at all, with its gentle hills and long plain, unobtrusive vegetation, and slightly faded colors. I remember my fellow passengers in the bus, conversations about a music festival in Kraków, and a little shop at the entrance to Oświęcim, full of objects that had nothing to do with the memorial site, cheaply priced silver, necklaces, rings, crosses, maybe other items I am no longer seeing clearly now. Everyone who had already been in Poland had brought back silver. "Buy silver!" was the motto of the day. It's easy to acquire a taste for these shops, and some of the ladies in the bus had brought irons and hair curlers to sell at a profit here in Poland. I remember my growing desire to buy something, anything, a simple chain necklace, for instance, although I really didn't need one, while struggling with feelings of shame to be thinking about money and profit here at this gate; after all, I was from a good family, which in our case meant that we reined in our yen for profit, which wasn't hard for us to do, since we had no money, and this conferred dignity on us and confirmed our sense of decency. But a new era had dawned, and our moral norms, which were carved out for eternity, no longer applied. If I didn't buy the necklace, I would surely come to regret passing up the opportunity to join in and be part of the group, to be one of the people who could buy because there was finally something to buy, and if everyone did it, it was surely a good investment. *Investment* was one of those brand-new words, so it couldn't be so bad to buy a silver chain here, at the entrance to Oświęcim, Auschwitz. That was not an immoral deed; it was in keeping with the times to be able to afford something mundane, as a sign of the victory over fascism, for instance. Still, the more I tried to convince myself of that, the more I felt torn apart and overcome with the feeling that pragmatism was inappropriate here. I think I recall holding my breath and opting for a compromise by buying three such chains as presents, as though their being presents jettisoned the question of good and evil. One for Mama, one for my best friend, and one just in case. I wound up keeping the last one for myself until a kind of unease impelled me to lose it; part of me must have wanted to let it go, yet I had a tinge of regret. Even Karl Marx wrote about the chains you lose on the path to freedom.

Once I'd purchased my three chains and was standing at the gate to Oświęcim, my memory ground to a halt. From this moment on, I do not recall anything. I have tried again and again to make my memory slip through the gate, just to have a look around, but it does not work. I was there, but didn't retain any sense of what I experienced, and I didn't reemerge until the next day, when we came to a lovely small town in the south of Poland, with a picturesque marketplace and *kościół*, a newly built, starkly modern church. I regained my composure at the sight of the young priest, whom I regarded as a creature unknown to me and all of science, as though he was the first person I had ever seen, as though I had just emerged from his rib, and as though he could not know that I belonged to his postdiluvian species. I beheld his sharp nostrils, his eyes, with their fan-like lashes, gazing upward to the Virgin Mary, his hands with their long, exaggeratedly decorous fingers, as though seeing everything human, the sum total of anatomy, for the very first time, though for some reason known only to God he was covered up by the cassock, and when he told us in a soft, impassioned voice about his new congregation, I couldn't concentrate on his concerns, so beautiful he was, beyond all measure. Had I been capable of concentration, I would have had to let in my memory of yesterday, the word itself and what it stands for, how to concentrate people and oneself; instead something within me asked what celibacy and the will of God are about, if I am so attracted to him. I clearly remember having a firm belief in God at the very moment when I was confusing beauty with desire, a belief made possible by my having forgotten something, but I did not know what exactly.

My fellow passengers from Kiev (then considered Russians in Poland) were now adorned and equipped with all manner of silver, and uncharacteristically quiet. There was no chatter or chitchat, but I heard sensible questions about God, Communists, and economic reform. Their solemnity showed that they had not entirely awakened from their nightmare; its spectral images were still galloping on long thin legs in front of their eyes.

Of course I know that we must have gone through this gate, I know what is written on this gate, the way I know what two plus two is, how "Frère Jacques" goes, or the Lord's Prayer, although I don't know that one well. I know well enough what the gate says and that I hate work so much because of it, even the word, *Arbeit*, which will never, with any coin or poem, buy its freedom from this verse, this curse, and that is why I just can't find any outlook on work, because I always wonder where this *Arbeit* will take me, for it's true what it says about freedom here, and there is no solution to that. I know how the paths run, I know what there is to see, what I could have seen there, because I saw the barracks, the containers like those for wholesale goods, and the entire site several times later, often enough to emblazon the place in my memory, but I recall nothing from that particular day.

I have tried to paste later impressions over this amnesia, which seemed to me like a thick pane of frosted glass, but nothing stayed in place, everything vanished like last year's foliage, and I saw only a golden autumn day with a mixed woodland at the edge of a painting.

Ariadne's Thread

Many years have gone by since my babushka Rosa died, but I still keep finding her hairpins, the black Soviet hairpins made of some flexible metal I can't put a name to, which have disappeared from the market with the collapse of the Soviet empire; maybe the raw material was produced in one of our republics, but the pins themselves in another one and then packaged somewhere in Asia, only to be transported back to the center, because everything was manufactured according to planned economic capriciousness. I find Rosa's hairpins in all cities of the world, in hotels, at modern train stations, in train corridors, and in the apartments of strangers, as though Rosa had been there shortly before me, as though she knew that I had lost my way and was showing me how to get home with her hairpins—even though she had never traveled abroad.

During the last years of her life, Rosa wrote her memoirs incessantly and in great haste, in pencil on white paper. The paper quickly turned yellow, as though anticipating its natural aging process, but Rosa's loss of sight was quicker. She didn't number the pages; she simply piled them up. Did she sense that there was no point in putting them in order if the individual lines couldn't be made out anyway? She often forgot to move on to a new sheet and wrote several pages' worth on the same piece of paper. One line ran into the next, and another one lay atop earlier writing like waves of sand on the beach, obeying a force of nature, tangled up in the interlaced and interwoven pencil scribblings.

Rosa fought off her blindness with her scrawl, lacing together the lines of her world as it slipped away. The darker it grew, the more densely she squeezed her writing onto the pages. Some passages were as inextricably intertwined as matted wool; the prices of potatoes in the late 1980s were knotted together with tales from the war and fleeting encounters. Here and there a recognizable word would seep through the woolen thicket: *ailing, Moscow, lifeblood.* For years, I thought that the texts could be deciphered—in America there are devices that can unscramble lines like these—until I understood that Rosa's writings were not intended for reading, but rather for holding on to, a thickly woven, unbreakable Ariadne's thread.

She sat in our apartment building on Ulitsa Florentsii, using the windowsill as a table. She saw as little outside as inside, and she wrote.

The only things I still write by hand are telephone numbers, which I enter into a small telephone book decorated with Leonardo da Vinci's handwriting. I bought it years ago in Florence, and whenever I look at Leonardo's refined flourishes, the mark of an era in which people still believed that man was the measure of all things, I always think of Babushka's illegible pencil scribblings.

Rosa's hands, which were always animated by her use of sign language, didn't rest even in retirement. She wanted to cook but wasn't able to, because she couldn't see, and her hands now adhered to different principles. She had spent her entire life with the deaf, she spoke sign language every day, her students called Rosa *Mi-ni-a-tur-na-ya-mi-mi-ka*, miniature mimic, as though that was her name, as though they had counted the syllables of her full name Ro-sa-li-ya-A-si-li-yev-na, translated them into sign language, and then back into spoken language, so that we could understand it as well. An elderly teacher from Rosa's school told me that she had the most beautiful yet bashful signs and gestures of all the hearing members of that community.

When I knew Rosa, she was almost blind. She could hardly make out shapes, and when I came into the room, she took me

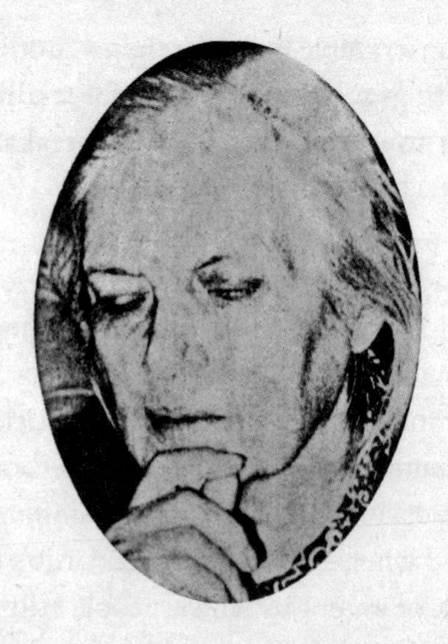

for my father or my brother. Never for my mother, her daughter, because my mother was seldom at home. Rosa had joined an association for the blind, and now she went throughout the city bringing other blind people food rations that were distributed by the association: a scrawny blue chicken, a bag of buckwheat, some condensed milk, and a can of sprats. For a long time I failed to understand why she was helping other people who in many cases were not nearly as blind as she, and no one helped her.

Once I watched her crossing the street, unable to see the traffic lights and cars, yet she had her eye on the secret destination that the other pedestrians were oblivious to, the blind and their food packages. She rushed out onto the road as though taking the stage. Before I could cry out, she was already in the middle of an incessant stream of traffic. The cars slowed down, as though guided to a gentle stop by an invisible hand, no sound of screeching, as though we had briefly relocated to the world of the deaf. Rosa clearly had angels watching over her. How she found the stops, numbers, addresses, entryways, floors, apartments, and people remains a mystery to me to this day.

Rosa was independent and stubborn. She never let anyone help her—it did not even occur to her that she might need help. She secretly saved up money for her own burial, the way many old people do to avoid being a burden to others, even after their deaths. Then came perestroika, prices shot up like the giants in our fairy tales, and Rosa's savings were wiped out.

Each time the hand of some gauge, unknown to us, struck a certain hour, Babushka headed down to the bakery. She bought a quarter loaf of bread and hid it under her pillow. That's how to outwit death: get hold of a crust of bread, and death can't catch you. The older she got, the deeper she sank back into the war. My mother was horrified every time she found one of these partial loaves, the expression of a widespread war syndrome without a known remedy.

I remember Babushka spending hours in front of the television, off to the left side, close to the screen, without glasses, because glasses no longer helped. Her profile was projected onto the flickering black-and-white image on the set. I never watched TV without her, and even years later, whenever I watch a program or go to the movies, I envision her silhouette, as though I fused it onto my optic nerve long in the past. She sang along to "The Internationale" in front of the television, *No higher being will save us / No God, no kaiser, no tribune. / To wrest us from our misery / We alone must do it soon!*

In Russian we were even more united in our misery, she firmly believed, and I believe her to this day.

As cumbersome as her increasing blindness made everyday life, it seemed to bestow a mark of honor that spared Rosa from deafness. Her sense of hearing grew keener and more refined, to the point that she heard voices that had faded away long ago. The less she could see, the more she sang the world of her youth back into life.

Rosa wanted to become an opera singer or to work at the operetta. She loved to dance, and as a young woman she often stole out of the house and away from the family's altruistic deaf-mute work to go to the operetta all on her own. She became a speech therapist and teacher of the hearing-impaired, dancing and singing for her students whenever she could. At the age of seventy-five, she still entertained me with her favorites: *Der Zigeunerbaron*, *Die Fledermaus*, *Die Bajadere*, and, above all, Verdi.

Why am I guilty for falling in love with Alfredo, she sang, in the odd Russian translation of "L'amore d'Alfredo perfino mi manca." Years later I found out that this was Violetta's aria from *La Traviata*. I was taken aback every time; Rosa sang so passionately, and this passion of my babushka, who had lived without a man for forty years, seemed so strange to me, and so palpable. Rosa knew dozens of Italian arias in Russian; she accompanied herself, singing and playing blind on the black piano, which stood in my room.

Rosa and her older daughter, Lida, had taught deaf-mute children; my mother and I no longer did, yet we retained the gestures, the motions of our hands. We worked our hands while speaking, as though our spoken language was itself nothing to speak of and incomplete without this accompaniment. Raising one hand or the other, folding our fingers together, small discordant movements without purpose or aim, at odds with themselves, stringing up ornaments in the air, we descendants accompanied ourselves with gestures. No one—not even we ourselves—understood the chords we were creating. We no longer played the piano, and little by little we unlearned the language of our hands and fumbled in the void.

When Rosa was old and no longer taught—I never saw her communicating with anyone in sign language—she would make beautiful movements, for no particular reason, at the dinner table on Ulitsa Florentsii, as though she was actually from Italy, and she continued these movements while wielding her knife and fork, often resulting in cutlery falling on the floor and knives flying through the air. Where others inherited silver cutlery, we inherited clumsiness in handling utensils of stainless steel. When Aunt Lida, Rosa's daughter, stopped working at the school for the deaf-mute, she took up smoking, and reined in her flailing hands with a cigarette and match. In. Out. Relax! Lida's daughter, Marina, was always knitting, not the motions of knitting in the air, like the deaf and their teachers, but sweaters, socks, skirts. She knitted everything, even bikinis, while I sat empty-handed over the computer keyboard.

But the most important thing about Rosa was her legs, my mother said. Rosa was proud of her legs, and it must be said that of all the women in our family, she had the loveliest. My babushka's legs were exquisite. She was fleet-footed, even in the hospital shortly before her death, and showed the nurses how to do the Charleston when they came to air out the room and Rosa had to get up despite her pain—she was only able to lie flat or dance. My mother was visiting and watched her mother dance; Rosa had been strictly forbidden to dance after her heart attack, and everyone knew that. My mother told me that Rosa gave a speech in front of all the patients, talking about the 1920s in Moscow and how she learned to dance, and while dancing she chatted about the New Economic Policy and how she had been present at Trotsky's speech in Molokokoopsoyuz, the Milk Cooperative Association, and how he had brought a cow onto the stage, well, maybe he wasn't the one to do it, my mother mused, but someone else, while Trotsky gave his speech, and I supposed that the Charleston reminded Rosa of Trotsky and his cow as she deftly danced her way into world history.

The legs of the women in our family grew worse with every succeeding generation. They were literally degenerating, my mother said—and she meant it seriously, although she enjoyed joking around—because the women in our family had spent centuries standing in front of their students six days a week, their legs bowed and their feet flattened into swans' feet, my mother said, evidently believing in both Darwin's evolution and Ovid's metamorphoses, and alarmed at what would become of me.

My grandfather Vasily can be seen in the photograph, a handsome man with a narrow face and finely chiseled features. He is leaning on his left knee; the table is covered with a heavy fringed cloth and a basket of roses. Rosa is dancing jauntily on the table, to something from a Kálmán operetta, "The beauty, the beauty, the beauty from the cabaret." I cannot alter anything in this picture, just edge the roses to the side. This was a marriage proposal, we were told, a basket full of roses and Rosa, the speech therapist, on the table.

When her chest pain grew more intense and Rosa called out the names Anna and Lyolya, her mother and her sister who had walked toward their deaths on Bolshaya Zhitomirskaya, my mother sent me a telegram in Leningrad. Rosa died on one of the top floors of the clinic. Ten minutes after her death, my mother went up to the window and saw me dashing across the huge courtyard down below, leaving tracks in the snow that had fallen overnight, like a bird, she said.

The Last Mother

After months of going from place to place to flee the war, my grandmother Rosa found work in a small town named Kinel-Cherkassy in the South Ural region. The head of the district authority entrusted her with two hundred children, and asked Rosa to set up, run, and manage an orphanage, an orphanage for two hundred half-starved children from Leningrad; none of them could die. The head of the district authority wanted to add something, my mother told me, but he choked on his words, then he promised my grandmother help, yet something remained unspoken, something like *otherwise . . . execution*. Maybe these words simply hung in the air like an old habit, a wartime routine, because even the famous phrase "Not a single step back! Moscow is behind us!" hinted at this menace. The words *otherwise execution* were at the tip of your tongue; you had to hold back so they didn't just tumble out of your mouth like the cawing of a crow. Maybe the head of this authority merely wanted to say that the children were weak and their lives were in jeopardy if Rosa did not make haste.

And so, in a wartime command, Rosalia Krzewina-Ovdiyenko, former director of the school for deaf-mutes in Kiev, became the head of an orphanage in the Urals for two hundred children who had lost their parents in the Siege of Leningrad. She had moved quickly, and everyone had helped. Military units heading to the front gave the children parts of their rations, and nearby kolkhozy and the local populace helped out with odds and ends. Everyone was hungry. The children were weak, some already in an advanced stage of hunger, *distrofiki* who had escaped from the Siege of Leningrad through the Road of Life across the frozen Lake Ladoga. None of Rosa's orphans died.

I cannot help but think of the twists and turns of fate, of chance occurrences in space and time. Back then, Janusz Korczak, the neighbor and colleague of Rosa's father, Ozjel, had also been evacuated in Warsaw, also with two hundred orphans—this, too, was a wartime command. Janusz Korczak was offered the chance to save himself, without the children.

During World War I, in Kiev, Janusz Korczak had begun writing his book, called, in the German translation, *How You Should Love a Child*. In the Polish there is no *should*; it's called

How to Love a Child, only three words in the original: *How Love Child*.

Korczak began his book in Kiev, on the street where my grandmother later lived, and again they were neighbors in space and time without knowing it. He was writing in Kiev because World War I had brought him into my city, and then he went back to Warsaw. If my great-grandfather Ozjel and my grandmother Rosa had gone back then, they and their orphanages, their orphans, and their own children would have become neighbors of Janusz Korczak, with the further destinations that this implies.

Rosa's most important task as the director was to scare up food. She had to take from the half-starved to give to the starving. She traveled through the villages by day and by night to gather supplies from the local residents. Once she was almost shot. In a rare stroke of luck, she was given two barrels of oil for the children at a kolkhoz that was quite some distance away. When she returned with the wagon in the night, one barrel was empty, but the papers said "two full barrels." The discrepancy meant that she would face a war crimes tribunal for theft. No one believed that Rosa was capable of stealing, but the law of war outweighed beliefs. Lida, Rosa's older daughter, my mother's big sister, who was fifteen at the time, persuaded those responsible to retrace the route, and after dozens of miles they found a trail of leaked oil.

Slowly the children regained their strength and their senses. Now it became apparent that they were little musicians and dancers, evacuated at the behest of the Pioneers' Palace in Leningrad, where they received their instruction, and they were accompanied by their music and ballet teachers. There were no ballet slippers, so poverty dictated modernity; the children danced barefoot and unrestrictedly, floating through the wide corridor of the orphanage in self-made capes. They put on concerts for the neighbors and the military.

Air Force Reserve Unit Number 5 had more on hand than other divisions, and shared its supplies with the orphanage. Sometimes the pilots played with the children; they missed their own children, and the children missed their fathers. My mother had two beautiful dresses, made of dark red and dark blue silk. Her father had brought them from Lithuania, where he had gone in 1940 to buy cows. Lithuania had just been conquered by the Soviet Union. Rosa took these dresses with her for her daughter when she fled from Kiev in late July 1941. They had no winter clothes with them; maybe they thought they'd be back by the winter, or maybe they were in too much of a hurry to think anything at all.

Rosa, who was then thirty-six years old, did not hear anything from her husband for two years. She was convinced that all were united in misery, and kept her personal needs to herself. She lived in the hall of the orphanage with her two daughters, where the rehearsals also took place between dance, song, and orchestra recitals; they were separated from the art by a thin curtain.

Were these children truly orphans, or were they just called orphans because they had been evacuated without their parents? Had someone gone to the trouble of looking for their parents? Or were they certain that the parents were dead? It

in the park. Then I rambled through the long new streets, where the faceless pale gray high-rises resembled antediluvian creatures with empty eye sockets. The old Warszawa was no longer there. Somewhere at the end of one of these long streets, I saw dilapidated old buildings that looked like open books, naked, facing outward to the sky and the people, frozen in the sun. They were largely demolished; only the spines and covers were still standing, their contents ripped out. The frontispieces showed traces of the lives of others, an inverted intimacy, small colorful squares made up of bedrooms, living rooms, and kitchens, a variety of wallpapers all with some sort of writing on them, which I started to decipher, reading all the more slowly the more I understood, until I saw that the walls were covered with countless expressions of hate for the very people who were no longer there. I would not have pictured such a thing in this city, in the capital of my first country beyond my own, my grandmother's hometown, on the stricken, defenseless buildings. My gaze groped through the expanses of the nonexistent rooms without understanding why I was spending such a long time looking at the desecrations, why I was staring at this gaping nakedness, as though an exhibitionist had suddenly opened his coat in a sunny park and there was no refuge from this unwanted encounter. How could I avert my gaze, and where else could I train it, in this place, once the most Jewish city in Europe?

I roamed about in this city with its newly built history and bought a vinyl record not far from the Chopin monument, out of sheer surprise at its jacket, which featured a Magen David—a term for the six-pointed Star of David I had just recently learned. The record sleeve read something like *Piosenki Żydowskie Europy wschodniej*. I transcribed the Polish words into Russian, and now I'm translating them into German as Jüdische Lieder aus Osteuropa (*Jewish Songs from Eastern Europe*). The Magen David was sprawled across the cover as matter-of-factly as our country sprawls across the map from Europe to the Pacific Ocean. I examined it the way I might watch an unknown animal that was on the verge of moving; I felt each of the six points, every corner, every angle. Throughout our lives we had drawn five-pointed stars, the ones on the earth and those resplendent in the sky, the stars of our Kremlin, as the old song said. There was also a song that had one star talking with another, which was usually sung when setting out alone, but none of those stars had six points. Never before in my endlessly extended native country had I encountered a Magen David as a sign or an object.

The six-pointed star surprised me, but not because I had always wanted to see a Magen David; I didn't even know one *could* wish for that. My wish was bereft of content, torn out by the roots, like the contents of the rooms of those abandoned houses. I was surprised and abashed at the sight of this Magen David, which was meticulously painted in dark blue on a white background, with a colorful dove in the middle.

Back in Kiev, I played the record, and my grandmother, who spoke with a slight Polish accent throughout her life—I remember the word *cacki*, said with a *ts*, Polish for nugget, which Rosa used to describe my junk, the useless things, *cacki*, like a sucking candy, a *ledenets*, with the chirping *ts*—my grandmother, who, as far back as I can recall, and as far back as my mother can recall, had never said a word in Yiddish, all of a sudden began to sing boisterous songs in a drifting minor key, first following and pursuing the words, then in tempo with them, and suddenly, merrily and swiftly, ahead of them, and I listened to her with the same incredulity I had felt when seeing the Magen David on the record. If there was no perestroika, if I had not gone to Poland, if this record had not existed, this sealed window of her early childhood would never have opened up to us, and I never would have been able to understand that my babushka came from a Warsaw that no longer exists; whether I like it or not, we are from that lost world, which my grandmother, who was already going from us, stepping down, recalled at a final boundary, at the edge.

As though she was caught in the act of recollection, her time stretched out and took hold of Rosa, and the record made it reach out to me and revive her memories, which, it appeared, had been thoroughly silenced and submerged, just like what may have been her mother tongue once, which we and even she herself had forgotten. Since encountering these songs, which my babushka sang along to while skipping about comically and clumsily in her seat—something I'd never seen her do before—I've been spending all my time mulling over the infinite variants of our lot in life, which could have been expressed in very different songs. What might have been, how about if, supposing it hadn't happened, or what would have developed if they had stayed in Warsaw in 1915 or emigrated to America, all of them?

Then I, too, skipped about comically and clumsily, like a needle on a worn record, skipped over the whole war like a realm not subject to my liberating fantasies, and wound up in the 1970s setting of my childhood, which my parents would have been able to leave. But they stayed to preserve actions and objects that are long since obsolescent and no longer on the market.

Divining Rod

My grandmother Rosa would not have understood my brother or me. When he was in his late twenties, he learned Hebrew, I German. He turned to Orthodox Judaism, out of the blue, as we all thought, and I fell in love with a German man. Both options were equally far removed from the way Rosa envisioned life. His Hebrew and my German—these languages changed our paths in life: *Enter at your own risk.* We were a Soviet family, Russian and nonreligious; Russian was the proud heritage of everyone who knew the meaning of desperation, in light of the fate of our own homeland. As the poet says, *Only you give me comfort and support, o you great, mighty, true, and free Russian language,* and today I hear in these words the German carol *O du fröhliche, o du selige.* We were no longer defined by our living and dead relatives and where they resided, but by means of our languages. When my brother started learning Hebrew in order to devote his life to Judaism, he plunged into the language without any fear of having gotten off to a late start, with the eagerness of a neophyte, without knowing what he was doing, and he recaptured the entire tradition, including the forgotten lore of the past. My choice was unreflective, but logical. With these languages, my brother and I together balanced out our provenance.

My German, still taut with unattainability, kept me from falling into a routine. I paid back my past in this language I acquired relatively late in life, as if counting out small change but with the ardor of a young lover. I coveted German because I wasn't able to merge with it, driven by an unrealizable longing, a love that knew neither object nor gender nor addressee, because there were only sounds, and they could not be captured, so wild they were and unattainable.

I threw myself into the study of German as though carrying on the battle against muteness, because German, *nemetskiy*, is in Russian the language of the mute. The Germans for us are the mute, *nemoy nemets*; the German cannot speak at all. For me, this German was a divining rod in the search for my family members who had taught deaf-mute children how to speak over the course of centuries, as though I had to learn the mute German so that I could speak, and this desire was inexplicable even to me.

I wanted to write in German, come hell or high water, I wrote, sagging under the weight of the swelling linguistic fodder, like a cow and an unborn calf all in one, bellowing and mooing, giving birth and being born, worth all the effort, with my untranslatable lodestars pointing the way as I wrote and lost my bearings on the stealthy paths of grammar—one writes the way one breathes—and I always sought to reconcile somberness and solace, hoping this reconciliation could send a taste of ocean breeze my way.

Often I entrenched myself in the language, with the right of the occupying power, I coveted that right, as though I had to storm the fortress, heave my entire body into the loophole, *à la guerre comme à la guerre*, as though my German were the precondition for peace, the death toll was considerable, and the losses meaningless and merciless, as is typical in our country, but if even I am writing in German, then in fact nothing and no one is forgotten, and even poetry is possible, and so is peace on earth.

My German, truth and illusion, the language of the enemy, was an outlet, a second life, a love that does not leave if it does not get, a gift and a goad, as if I had set a bird loose.

The Train

In July 1941, when my mother left her hometown of Kiev, she was not even six years old. Everything she told me about her childhood revolved around the war. She had memories of what had come before, but in the war she had found something to satisfy her hunger for grand feelings, her natural longing for justice. War became her gauge for everything that followed.

The war forced her to part from her father, take leave of her childhood, and embark on her first arduous journey through the vast country. When the fighting was over, her grandfather was no longer alive, her grandmother Anna and her aunt Lyolya had been killed, and her father, Vasily, had vanished. It seemed to me that her memories of what came before—the trips to the movies with her grandfather, the Ginsburg house at the end of her street, which was then the tallest building in the city—existed for the sole reason of future visiting, because the war shed light in both directions; what came before no longer existed, and memory became the only proof of the past.

She told me about the war again and again, even though there was hardly anything to tell beyond a few stories, but she used these primary colors to paint all the stories of her life that lay ahead. Her war became mine, as did her distinction between the before and the after, and at some point it was no longer possible for me to distinguish her war from my dreams and to let her recollections rest in the storehouse of my memory.

Time and again, I woke up in an overcrowded train, with the people perched on sacks, my six-year-old mother, her sister Lida, my babushka Rosa, all huddled in a corner of the cattle car. The journey had been going on for days. My mother lay on the floor of the car, which was covered with a scant bit of straw. She had the measles. The phrase *cattle car* did not weigh on my mind, because I knew that they were traveling in the other direction, not in the direction of death, but toward the unknown.

My mother told me that her mother, Rosa, seized every opportunity to get water, which was possible only when the train stopped near a station and not in the middle of an open field. The trains came to a halt without notice, and they started up unannounced as well. Hundreds of mothers got out. One time the train started moving while Rosa was still standing at the well with her jug.

I'm picturing us all at once: my babushka, my mother as a child, her sister, myself. Throw away the jug! Run! But it's as though the jug and Rosa are fused together. She runs, the water has all spilled out, for a moment it is as though all is lost, as though she'll never catch up to the train, but when all seems lost apart from the jug in her hand, she suddenly reaches the train, as in a film cut, as though we had looked away for an instant. What other explanation is there for a person who, about to give out, is still faster than an accelerating train? Through the open sliding door of the car the other women stretch out their hands to her and manage to pull up my mother's mother, my babushka, who is just thirty-five years old. First I see the scene in fast motion, then it slows down, as if something could be explained by slowing the event so that the turning point becomes visible.

My mother was convinced for the rest of her life that they would have lost each other forever if Rosa hadn't caught up to the train, and that she herself would have died of measles in the train, despite her sister's efforts.

It's the same dream that keeps repeating is a line in the song my brother used to sing, in a quick, scudding rhythm with his guitar, *I dream that I'm left behind the train.* There were other trains in our childhood, such as the "armored train on the reserve track," because we were all "peaceful Soviet people," but that was not my train. My train was gone, and I had to catch up to it.

Again and again the train starts moving, and I see the mouths open wide, the mute screams as in a silent movie, as though all senses have been transformed into movement, as though there was only something to see and nothing to hear. And again the young woman in the light dress runs a relay race with the jug to pass it along, because without water there is no surviving, her legs ablaze like those of a cartoon character, the woman is younger than I am today. *I can run faster,*

Babushka!, and even though I don't want to, I run, I run for her, every time I recall this scene, I run for her, it is not a memory, I run for her life. While I'm running, I wake up, I run, and the train is picking up speed. From above I see the outstretched hands, I am the one above, no, wait, my Rosa is. I am standing down below, the train zooms past and is swallowed up by the gray landscape.

Facebook 1940

Sometimes I had the feeling that in picking my way through the rubble of history, I was gradually losing the sense not only of my search, but of my entire life. I wanted to bring far too many of the dead back to life and had not thought through a strategy to do so. I read random books, I traveled through random cities, and in the process made pointless, even false movements. But maybe—and this is only a bold assumption on my part—I stirred up the ghosts of the past with all this moving around, touching a tender membrane somewhere in the lowest layer of heaven, one that a human being might still reach. And I thought that this is where my mother, a headstrong teacher, had always whiled.

This time the phone was ringing. New Year's Eve, 2011, in Kiev. My mother went to answer it.

My name is Dina, an old woman said, I've heard that you're collecting everything you can about School #77 in Kiev. I graduated from that school in 1940. I'm calling from Jerusalem.

It had been quite some time since we had received a call that brought us back to 1940. It was like a cold wind from the past, from the beyond, and Jerusalem, the way station for this connection, served as proof. My mother stood transfixed, the receiver in hand, and could only say in a hoarse, but firm voice, Yes, I'm listening.

The telephone was set on speaker.

The New Year's Eve guests fell silent.

We left Kiev right at the beginning of the war, Dina said resolutely. We were evacuated to Dagestan. In the 1970s we emigrated from there to Israel. I never returned to Kiev. I just found one of my girlfriends from my 1940 graduating class on Facebook. She told me that you're looking for us. Yes, I'm eighty-eight years old, I can use a computer with my daughter's help. Are you an archivist?

No, I'm a history teacher, my mother said, and went on to explain that she'd been working in this school for forty years and was trying to reconstruct its history, although I'd say she was newly constructing it. A long time ago, I put on a play with a group of students, she said, about the graduates who had gone off to the front the very day after their graduation party, the first day of the war. We had found some of them and brought them onto the stage.

Dina skirted the issue and listed the names of her classmates, then those of all the teachers and some parents.

She remembered all of them, seventy years after her graduation.

After the war, as the survivors slowly came back to Kiev, from the front or from the evacuation, no one knew anything about Dina. A quarter of the class had died in the war, and at some point people stopped looking for one another. Dina was Jewish, and could have perished in the Babi Yar ravine or elsewhere. Sometimes there was no search, because people were sure. But Dina lived.

Where did you live in Kiev? my mother asked.

Not far from the school, on Institutskaya Street.

When my mother heard this street name, she grew frantic. Where exactly?

At the corner of Karl Liebknecht.

In the gray building at the corner? Across from the pharmacy?

Yes! said Dina, the first doorway on the left.

But we lived there too! my mother shouted.

There weren't any Petrovskiys in our building, Dina replied.

But I'm Ovdiyenko!

Svetochka! Dina shouted.

Everyone there was silent, as though they knew. My father was the first to let out a little sob. My mother had been called by someone who was already grown up when she herself was still a child. There was no one else left from that generation.

Dina really had been my mother's neighbor, thirteen years older than Svetochka. She recalled all the members of our family and the neighbors from the prewar building.

After rattling off this long list, she said, Thank you, Svetochka.

What for? Svetochka asked.

And Dina expressed her thanks, seventy years later, for the

way my grandmother Rosa, who was then the director of the deaf-mute school, entrusted her own students to her when she was looking for work. This set the course of her lifelong career; after the war Dina became a teacher of the deaf, and her daughter later followed in her footsteps. They first taught in Dagestan, then in Israel, and her daughter's children also became teachers of the deaf and speech therapists, as had some of the great-grandchildren. Because of you and yours, Svetochka.

Then Dina said that she remembered the death of my great-grandfather, Ozjel Krzewin, in 1939. I heard him falling onto the floor, and I ran upstairs, sometime that autumn. I was four years old, my mother said, and I still recall that all the grown-ups were flabbergasted when I said, Leave him alone, he's tired. And Dina said, That's right, you said that!

CHAPTER 3

MY BEAUTIFUL POLAND

Polsha

I bore my chalice safely through a throng of foes.

—JAMES JOYCE

When I was growing up in Kiev, the country next door, Poland, our nearest neighbor, Polsha in Russian, was an unattainable, beautiful foreign land. Graceful women lived there, the men had fine manners, people believed in God, in spite or because of communism—maybe they always had—and everyone went to the soaring Gothic churches. You could even buy chewing gum in Poland.

I often announced, for no good reason, that my grandmother Rosa, Rosalia, was born in Warsaw, as though this piece of news harbored an act of defiance. I was proud that my grandmother came from Poland; it was a trump card in a game that no one was playing with me. Some of my classmates had distinctly Polish names, such as Studzinski and Shtshegelskaya, but we were Soviet children all the same, with the same haze surrounding our family histories, which may have been the very reason for our sameness. I was proud, as though I myself had a whiff of Polish grace, manners, and faith, as though I, too, could strike the attitude of noble opposition, demeaned but never subjugated, *jeszcze Polska nie zginęła*, Poland is not yet lost, and despite knowing full well that I would never belong, that back then, in 1905, when my grandmother came into the world, this part of Poland was governed by the Russian Empire and my family was Jewish. In the Soviet years of my life, I never played my Polish trump card, *kozyrnaya karta*, but saved it until it suddenly fell back into my hands in Warsaw.

When I met new people from Poland, I started by apologizing for the three partitions and then for the fact that in 1944 the Soviet army waited at the shore of the Vistula until the Warsaw uprising was subdued. I apologized to the modern Poles of Europe, whom I made prisoners of my conscience, I apologized for Katyń and for the uprising, as depicted in the film *Kanał*, because I knew yet couldn't alter a thing, I even apologized for the year 1981, as though I ought to have saved the *Solidarność* at the elfin age of eleven. We were to blame. Admitting my Soviet origin, I recognized the achievements of the Empire, but also knew it marched in step with suffering inflicted on others.

My father was in love with this poor Poland, with Polish poetry and the sound of the language, this Polsha, which was not yet lost, *jeszcze nie zginęła*. It was the epitome of femininity in our socialist world. My father read many books in Polish that hadn't been translated into Russian; he read James Joyce's *Dubliners* in kindred Polish, and he and his friends even read Russian books in Polish translation when they were inaccessible in their original. Something about his love baffled me. My father was a child of the war, one of the Chosen People, nearly all of whom had been murdered in his city of Kiev, and even more in Poland, yet he forgivingly grieved for Poland when contemplating the sewers, the Warsaw uprising, the Polish partitions, Katyń. He regarded the Polish tragedy as a source of anguish, as though he could fathom his own pain only in the pain of others, in an act of translation. He would have considered it indecent to let his grief fester within him. Many of his friends in Kiev who were drawn to Poland in the 1950s, 1960s, and later years were of Jewish descent and knew full well what had gone on in Poland, including the postwar era and the way survivors were treated. They never held it against the Poles, because they had the other Poland in their hearts, and when I asked my father how it was possible for them to love Poland so devotedly when Poland didn't love them back, he said, Love need not be requited.

Ozjel's Asylum

Ozjel Krzewin, the father of my grandmother Rosa, was a teacher, the director of a small boarding school for deaf-mute children in Warsaw. Most of the children were orphans. I knew the address of the family's home before World War I, the home where Rosa and her two siblings were born. The family and the orphans lived together. I pictured a modest but merry household, and a strenuous daily routine. That was not a profession but an obsession, and it ran throughout the family: Ozjel's six siblings had also founded schools for deaf-mute children, in Hungary, France, and Austria. But even my parents could not provide exact details about any of them. In search of Ozjel, I traveled due east from Berlin, to the Warsaw of prewar antiquity.

Ozjel was born in Vienna in 1870, one hundred years before me. I was proud of that as well—our family was from Vienna. As if by miracle, a Soviet employment record belonging to my great-grandfather survived at home, as well as a biographical note that indicated that he had been a teacher of the deaf-mute in Koło-Kalisz-Limanova-Warsaw-Kiev. After his father's death, he took over his school in Warsaw. His name was Ozjel, but I heard it as Asil or Asiliy, because in Russian an unstressed *o* is pronounced as an *a*. At first I thought that this name came from azaleas, perhaps because my grandmother's full name was Rosaliya Asiliyevna, or Rosaliya Asaliyevna, as some said. As I got older, I thought about this strange-sounding great-grandfather and his name, which offered me a background and sanctuary, Asiliy and his asylum, providing shelter, seclusion, refuge for all. I was descended from someone who tended to people that society had abandoned. The deaf-mute orphans were the dearest residents in Asiliy's asylum. Parents from Kraków, Vilnius, and Kiev sent their children to Ozjel's school in Warsaw.

> *We never expected our daughter to be able to write and say difficult Russian and Yiddish words after just 3 months. Even to write a letter! This appeal is addressed to all unfortunate parents. Fellow unfortunates, our hearts go out to you. Do send your poor deaf-mute children to the most outstanding teacher. The address is: O. Krzewin—Warszawa—Ciepła.*

He was considered a healer, even though he was only a teacher. The Hebrew newspapers wrote about Ozjel and his little school on Ulica Ciepła, and published letters of thanks. These letters cry out with the voices of exhausted parents; heavy-handed expressions of happiness gush out in their awkward formulations.

My pen is not capable of writing what I am feeling. No matter how long I would thank you, it would be slight in comparison to what you have done. I cannot express my jubilance on paper. I could not have imagined that my son would write and speak so soon! I saw deaf-mutes in your school who started to speak in a way that one could not recognize that they were deaf-mutes. I shed tears of joy when my child began to speak with me. I wish that God may help you so that you will always have good fortune.

This letter, from Kiev, is dated May 1914. Then the war came, and in 1915, Ozjel and his sister Maria were charged with spying for Austria and brought to Sedlecka Prison. Were they accused of hiding young men from the military? Or were deaf-mutes regarded as spies, as was common in wartime? Anyone who does not speak must be hiding something.

A few hours after being released from prison, Ozjel packed his bags and left Warsaw with his family—his wife, Anna Levi-Krzewina, and their three children, Rosa, Lyolya, and Arnold, who were nine, six, and two years old—and ten deaf-mute orphans from his school with their deaf-mute teacher, Abram Silberstein.

Ozjel had a son from his first marriage, my mother told me. Zygmunt must have been about sixteen years old when his father immigrated to Kiev. Fifteen years later, Zygmunt came to Kiev with his wife, Helena, Hela, to visit his father. My grandfather, Vasily, Rosa's husband, flirted with Polish Helena, but my mother could not tell me anything else about him.

In fleeing the war, hundreds of thousands of Poles came to Kiev and made it a lively Polish city for several years. Ozjel founded the first school for deaf-mutes, and when most of the refugees went back to Warsaw, he stayed on. He never set foot in Warsaw again. Ozjel started with his ten pupils from Warsaw; they all lived together in a house, as they had before.

They can all be seen in this photograph. On the right is Sil-

berstein, the deaf-mute teacher who had come from Warsaw with them. We may be the only ones who still know of his existence. He committed suicide in 1916, after falling in love with a girl who could speak. They wanted to marry, but her parents said no.

During World War I the school grew, and now also accepted children who were not congenitally deaf-mute. I read a visitor's report stating that in 1919 Ozjel found a girl at the edge of town, a "pogrom girl" it called her, as though that was an utterly normal term. A good many of the deaf-mute orphans came from pogrom families, according to an article about Ozjel's school that was published in *Proletarskaya Pravda.* There was no further clarification.

Later, the orphanage moved into a larger building on Bolshaya Zhitomirskaya, which was called Ulitsa Lvovskaya back then. Students, teachers, workers, and scholars came from Moscow and Leningrad to have a look at the school, some out of curiosity, some on behalf of the ministry of education. Thanks to these visitors, we know about the atmosphere, the teachers' dedication, and the children's abilities and open minds, as though they had come to life. At that time, sign language was no longer officially endorsed, but my relatives still used it. They employed deaf-mute teachers, and the older students helped instruct the younger ones.

Right in the middle of the city, the children kept chickens, rabbits, goats, a chestnut horse, and cows. There was also a peacock, a peacock in a Soviet school, a divine creature incompatible with any class theory, like the school itself. The peacock was beautiful, beauty was as important as proficiency, and the deaf children enjoyed the beauty of the hundred eyes in a manner that we can't, seeing its dazzling plumage, which covered the horizon, without hearing its disturbing shriek. They learned useful skills: they did their own sewing, made shoes for other orphanages, bound books and portfolios for private and government clients, and took in the beauty of the world in the process. They performed pantomimes, walked through the city, kneaded and created sculptures, and went to the opera, because even though they could not hear the sounds, they were so fascinated by what they saw that they painted pictures of Gounod's *Faust* for quite a long time. A report indicates that they also painted portraits of Karl Marx and his successors. The whole family pitched in: Ozjel's wife, Anna Levi, and their youngest son Arnold. Their eldest daughter, Rosa, my grandmother, had started working in the school at the age of sixteen, and maybe her love for opera inspired her to take the children to the ballet and the opera and afterward to dance and paint with them. She also seemed to believe in Karl Marx and his successors. A poster in the school read, "With our hearts, not with our ears, we hear Lenin's call to communism."

In the 1930s, the tone of the reports changed; visitors turned harsh and their assessments scathing. First there was an end to the prayers, to Hebrew and Yiddish, then to Ozjel's unconventional curriculum. Later sign language was prohibited; it was considered a visible feature of a minority, a closed society, and in the Soviet Union there were to be no more minorities. Every opportunity was open to internationalists, as one big family and in one big language. Ozjel tried to save his languages; he resisted, accepted compromises, negotiated. His daughter Rosa succeeded him as director.

He died in good time, as they say when speaking about this era, in early October 1939, of a heart attack, in a Kiev that was still peaceful. On September 1, Germany had invaded Poland. On September 17, Red Army troops converged on Poland from the other side. When Warsaw fell and Poland capitulated, Ozjel was heating water for his Sunday bath. Ozjel fell along with Warsaw, never having seen his Poland again.

Ulica Ciepła

I wanted to go to Warsaw, which was then in the Russian Empire, and is now in the European Union. Between the Warsaw of the present and the Warsaw of the past lies one of the most devastated cities of Europe. I wanted to go there, if only to smell the air.

As a Russian from Germany, I traveled to the Jewish Warsaw of my relatives, to Poland, to Polsha. My two languages, I felt, made me a representative of the occupying powers. As a descendant of battlers against muteness, I was ready for action, yet mute. I did not speak any of the languages of my ancestors: not Polish, not Yiddish, not Hebrew, not sign language; I knew nothing about the shtetl, or any prayers, I was a novice at all the disciplines in which my relatives were highly qualified. I used the Slavic languages I knew to divine the Polish, hunches stood in for knowledge, Poland was deaf, I was mute.

O. Krzewin. School for the Deaf and Mute, Ulica Ciepła 14, Warszawa.

Heinrich Schliemann did not recognize his Troy at first, because he had dug too deep. I traveled to a Warsaw that had existed two epochs earlier. To be able to see anything at all, I had to ignore the ruins that lay between me and the period one hundred years in the past.

All you need to do is mention the words *Warsaw* and *Jews* in the same breath, and everyone starts talking about the ghetto as though it were a mathematical operation: Warsaw plus Jews equals ghetto. Historians say ghetto, my friends say ghetto, the Internet barks out ghetto. I tried to bewail this state of affairs on the Internet, as though the Internet was the Wailing Wall of the nonbelievers, but there, too, I came up against the walls of the ghetto. In an attempt to fend off such references, I repeated that of course the ghetto was the most important thing, but I was looking for my history here, which started much earlier. My grandmother was born in Warsaw in 1905, my great-grandfather had a school for the deaf-mute here until 1915, and that was that. Yet the people I was talking to, those in the fields of Warsaw historiography and its well-equipped outposts in the Internet and in scholarship, were in the majority, and they all said ghetto. Ghetto here! Ghetto there! Ghetto up! Ghetto down! They glittered in their armor and dazzled my mind. Eventually I capitulated. My grandmother was born here. Right in the middle. Let's just say in the ghetto. There was no ghetto in 1905, and there isn't one now. There are banks where there was once a ghetto. The ghetto is everywhere.

When Ozjel left Warsaw, his mother and his sister Maria stayed behind. I'd never thought about it, but an idea began to take hold of me. When Ozjel died, in 1939, we never told his mother in Warsaw, who was already ninety-one. And then another idea flashed up. We sent packages to Warsaw, even in 1940; after that they were no longer accepted. How many years did I bear these two ideas within me until I heeded them?

We sent them packages. I sensed the magnitude of this short sentence, thinking the whole time what these packages from Kiev to Warsaw might have contained, whether they were still keeping kosher in the summer of 1940, when the ghetto was set up, and whether my relatives still kept kosher in Kiev, and how things were with kosher in Kiev, and what a cozy word *kosher* is, and whether it was still important to keep kosher in 1940, when the essential issue was just to eat, and I also thought about how our Jewishness is like these packages we can no longer peer inside. We say "Jewish," but never know what the word is filled with.

I found Ulica Ciepła on the map of the ghetto, then drew my own map. Six lines horizontally and six vertically, in the second column from the bottom, close to the middle, I made a cross for our house, Ciepła 14.

It was cold. Why do I always travel in the winter? The building developments seemed chaotic. The route through the ghetto: a department store, an office building, a health club, a Westin hotel, small shops, a hair salon, an Internet café, a bakery, a ruin from some time or other, another hotel. Who stays in all these hotels?

Again and again I walked up and down Ulica Ciepła. Of course I had known in advance that nothing remained of my area, yet in the course of my quest I moved back and forth like a pendulum, a measuring device like time itself, without slowing down, as though this back-and-forth would carry out a ritual that I discerned and devised myself, in the hope of making out the contours of the era. One spot smelled like bread, another like Internet connections. I could have gone into a restaurant to warm up, drink tea, and eat piroshki, to live, but I walked back and forth instead. I walked and walked and thought the old houses would come forward and the past would show me its countenance out of respect for my senseless effort. However, I wasn't miserable enough for that to happen.

At some point I grew so cold that I went into a supermarket and studied my ghetto map once again. I knew the new Ulica Ciepła by heart, yet I still did not know on which block my house had been. Across from me, well-dressed Poles were standing in line, doing their shopping while I was occupied with the vanished world that had once been the city of their ancestors as well, not only the city of some unrelated others.

I took to them, and I wanted them to take to me as well; I so hoped one of them would understand what I was seeking here.

Two Cities

As a tourist entering the city, you have to decide which catastrophe you are basing your visit on, Warsaw uprising or ghetto, as though there had been two Warsaws, and some people think that there really *were* two, separated by time and space.

In Stare Miasto, the Old Town, the buildings display plaques about the Warsaw uprising the way a war veteran displays medals, and there are so many of them that these plaques could be used to hold up not only the buildings in the center of town but all of Poland. Before the war, Warsaw was full of the Jewish faith, Jewish cooking, and the Yiddish language, unlike the Kiev of my childhood. Now the traces of this life seemed like alien elements. In 1939, when the war began, one million people lived in Warsaw, thirty-nine percent of them Jews. I never fail to be astonished that the murderers and those who commemorate the deaths always know precisely how to tally up the numbers. The thirty-nine changed everything for me. Once you get up to thirty-nine, it is no longer a matter of us and them, but you and your neighbors, I thought, every second or third person, you and me. In 1939, thirty-nine percent.

How should this substantial portion of the populace be commemorated? And how can one still live here? If Warsaw were to follow the example of Berlin and set a stumbling stone of memory into the sidewalk for every person who was taken away, the streets of Warsaw, large and small, would be paved with golden stones. The people and the other people, the victims and the other victims—there were always the others, no matter where one came from—Poles and Jews, Jews and Poles, and if they perished in Katyń, they were allowed to be Poles, but their wives and children remained Jews and lived in the ghetto.

Family Heritage

In the spot where I looked for the Jewish Genealogy & Family Heritage Center, there was a dark blue mirrored Peugeot skyscraper, an endless wall to the right, to the left, and upward. I moved back a few steps and studied the surface of the skyscraper as though I were taking an eye exam, and scanned the pane of glass for Family Heritage, until I discovered a Plexiglas plaque that only people schooled in these things would notice. I went closer and read it. This had been the site of the largest synagogue in Warsaw, built in such and such a year, blown up in such and such a year, and a photograph. On the ground floor, next to a supermarket and a car showroom, I found Family Heritage, and pulled open the heavy door.

The search went more quickly than I would have expected. I have it, Anna said, and showed me a chart on the computer. We were sitting close together at the table in the office, and after just a few seconds, we had the correct spelling for all the names. Ozjel Krzewin married Estera Patt in 1895, she explained to me, and in 1898 they had a son named Szymon, your Zygmunt. I had been at the institute for just ten minutes, and I already had new dates and a new name, Estera Patt, Ozjel's first wife. You're lucky, Anna said, that your family doesn't come directly from Warsaw. *Lucky*?

Hardly anything about Warsaw families has been preserved; all the archives were destroyed. The Christian population was registered twice—in the church and in the municipality—at birth, marriage, and death, but the Jews were registered only once, Anna explained, so the data for the Poles can be reconstructed in part, but for the Jews the loss was of course disastrous. I thought about this "of course disastrous"; not only had the people disappeared, but hardly anything remains to indicate that they had ever existed in the first place. Anna again made reference to my luck, as though there was something to gain in this game of chance, as though I were holding all the trump cards in my hand. It helps, she went on to say, that your family has a rare name.

The Krzewins were originally from the Kalisz region. She showed me the charts with lists of names of my presumptive relatives, dozens of Hawas and Ozjels, Rivkas and Bajlas, plus a Rajzla, an Icek, a Frajda, a Józef, a Natan, another Rajzla, and a Tobiasz. Krzewins from the Koło shtetl, in the vicinity of Kalisz.

Tobiasz Krzewin was a source of particular amazement to me. He was one of the first to be mentioned in the family charts, and his first child was born in the year that Joseph Haydn wrote *Il ritorno di Tobia*. My husband's name is Tobias. I knew the name only in a German context and had never thought of it in connection with Tevye the Milkman, the set of short stories by Sholem Aleichem, and the musical *Fiddler on the Roof.*

And then there were Zygmunt and Hela.

Here, here, I see both of them. Anna turned the screen toward me and I saw two death records from Yad Vashem. Maybe I had traveled to Warsaw for the sole purpose of accepting this Internet discovery from Anna's hands: Zygmunt Krzewin, born in Kalisz, in Warsaw during the war, deported to Lublin, shot dead in 1943. Hela Krzewina (Hammer), born in Kalisz, in Warsaw during the war, deported to Treblinka, date of death August 1942.

I still need to find my building, I quickly said to Anna. All of a sudden, everything seemed very plodding, moving in slow motion. Stara Warszawa. Anna was showing me a website, the Warsaw of the prewar period. Here is a photo of Ulica Ciepła, although not of the section you need.

Go over to Janek's, Anna said; he has everything.

eBay Now

Jan Jagielski was a good seventy years old and greeted me with the effusive politeness of a gentleman from the previous era. He led me into a spacious room of the Żydowski Instytut Historyczny: cabinets with thick glass doors and heavy frames, tables that stood on lions's paws, dark wood chairs, shelves with hundreds of files. I'm looking for Ulica Ciepła 14, I said, and recounted my story. Ciepła!, Janek said, I live around the corner. That was the poor side of town. He took a file off the shelf marked "Mirów District," and showed me photos of the area. He quoted Louis Aragon and murmured to himself in a mixture of French, Russian, and Polish. Suddenly he straightened up, as though about to award me an honor, and said, Here it is, the photo.

A great many people are on the street, some of them looking my way, full of fear, as though a danger was radiating from me, as though I were the photographer, a perpetrator. Stars of David. Here's the building. You're in luck, Janek said, that is the only photo.

I no longer understood how I ever could have imagined that I had been spared. Somehow I knew that my Polish relatives had all perished, Ozjel's siblings, his mother, Zygmunt, Hela, their family—how else could this have ended?—but I had never thought about them.

What sort of luck? I asked Janek.

I bought this photo on eBay, he said, in recent years eBay has been a good source, hundreds of photos, old people sell them before they die, or their children do. I bought this photo from a member of the Wehrmacht, for seventy euros, a good price.

The Rehearsal

When I went to a meeting in the evening with a Polish theater director who had just won the Golden Nike, the premier literary prize in Poland, for his play about a school class during the war, I ran into my neighbor from Berlin on the street, which would have been a nice coincidence if I hadn't just read a play that refers to *Neighbors*, a book about Polish and Jewish classmates who grew up together, lived together, and then turned on and killed one another, guess who killed whom, and just as I was thinking of the neighbors in the small Polish town with the unpronounceable name Jedwabne, and why people kill their neighbors, in a delirium, in the dark, in the heat of the moment, or with malice aforethought, suddenly there he was, standing in front of me, here in Warsaw, my neighbor who lives across the street from me in Berlin, with whom I like to stop for a chat every once in a while.

We're rehearsing here right now, my neighbor said; he is an opera singer and is named Tobias, like my husband and the ancestor I've just discovered. Tobias had a part in a Warsaw production of Xenakis's *Oresteia*, of all things. We were standing in the cold, surprised to be meeting up here. I wasn't sure what exactly we were rehearsing at this point, and I mentioned that I was looking into the subject of neighbors and how things may have been during the war, when everyone was the neighbor of everyone else, and he told me enthusiastically about the violence in the Xenakis opera, about the infinite chain of victims and casualties, Agamemnon kills his daughter Iphigenia, Iphigenia's mother Clytemnestra kills her husband Agamemnon when he returns from the Trojan War, and Orestes kills his mother Clytemnestra and is pursued by the Erinnyes, and then the percussion, the famous drumming scene, and how nice it was to run into each other, how nice and bye-bye, but as I walked along I heard the Erinnyes entering the city while darkness was falling.

Nike

Reading *Legends and Myths of Ancient Greece* as a child, I drew a gallery of the gods and heroes in pencil, each figure on its own sheet of paper. I pored through the small print of the myths attentively and so often that the glossy paper of the deluxe edition gradually dulled with my many fingerprints, the only identity card I had at the time. I left confirmation of my existence on the fields, cliffs, and seas of the ancient Greek world. At some point, my blood flowed onto the pages as well, with the first nosebleed of my life, and it was immediately soaked up by the Greek soil, lending the myths the terra-cotta color of ancient ceramics, as though I was on the scene of the Greek battles and attended my Soviet school only during the lulls in the fighting.

I drew all of Olympus and the surrounding area, I drew

Apollo, Athena, Zeus and Artemis, Hercules, Polyphemus, Odysseus, Pan with his flute, and even the fuzzy sheep. I was nine or ten years old, and I was thrown by how casually the gods and heroes displayed their bodies, their bare muscles, breasts, and genitals. I couldn't imagine that we or our adults would be capable of assuming these kinds of poses, in the everlasting repose of the pleasures of the flesh, not even when alone and unseen. I liked the distinctive nature of these inaccessible Greeks, but I did not know what to do with the sexual organs that were facing toward me, how to render them in my emerging gallery of the gods and heroes, until I hit upon a radical solution. I drew the gods and heroes with their backs to the viewer, as though they were turning away from us, as though I knew that the gods would leave us, displaying their divine attributes but not their human qualities.

Nike, the goddess of victory, was the only one in my gallery to survive all the intervening eras and governments. I still have that piece of paper today, a figure with a well-shaped behind and two wide wings, faceless, genderless, like an angel.

The Wrong House

I called my mother and tried to sum things up: Mama, I found Zygmunt, Ozjel's eldest son, and Helena, his wife, you know, the two who once came from Poland to Kiev for a short visit. Both are on the list of Yad Vashem. No mistake about it. It's on the Internet. No, not a trace of Ozjel's mother or Maria. Then I shook out all the Rivkas, Bajlas, Rajzlas, Iceks, Frajdas, Józefs, Natans, all our old-but-new relatives, as though they were emerging from a cornucopia, and did you know, Mama, that Ozjel's first wife was named Estera Patt? Yes, my mother said, of course, I know, she was mute, yes, in Ozjel's first marriage, he was married to a deaf-mute woman, she died quite early, I've told you that a thousand times. I couldn't believe it; she had never told me. But my mother insisted that she had told me about Estera Patt, several times. She insisted quite stubbornly, as though she had sung me a lullaby about my great-grandfather's first wife who had been deaf-mute, *Estera Patt was, mm-mm, mute, Estera Patt was mute.*

And then I said, Mama, can you believe it, I found the house, Ulica Ciepła, no, only the photo, and my mother said, Yes, unbelievable, really wonderful, but I'm sorry, I completely forgot that the house number you were looking for was 16 and not 14. Forgive me, Katenka, we wrote 14 everywhere, but the orphanage and the school and the apartment were actually at 16.

I felt dazed, as though I been both deceived and deceiver. How many people had I roused to look for my number 14, and now it was wrong, my house was no longer mine.

This photo of Ulica Ciepła 14 in 1940 with all the people who three years later would be dead, I would have to go back and tell Janek that we had found and gone through all that in vain, because my relatives had lived and worked in number 16 before World War I, take your dead back, please, you're standing in front of the wrong house in the wrong time.

I took another look at the picture. What luck! On the photo that Janek had bought on eBay a year earlier, *two* buildings could be seen, numbers 14 *and* 16. I studied their outlines on the ghetto map. They are both there. I have two houses and the people standing in front of them. I can't imagine that anyone else will come to Janek on the search for number 14, not even due to a mix-up.

Kozyra

Throughout the city there were posters for a casting call. I had already seen the word *casting* in the ghetto, on an announcement of an exhibition by the video artist Katarzyna Kozyra. The name Kozyra gave me a jolt: *kozyr'* is "trump" in Russian, and *kozyrnaya karta* is a trump card. I abandoned myself to my game of chance and took a deep breath. Never have I felt as perfectly lost as here in Warsaw; I thought in Russian, looked for my Jewish relatives, and wrote in German. I was lucky to be able to move in that space between languages, swapping words and switching roles and viewpoints. Who conquered whom, who was one of mine, who was one of the others, which shore is mine?

On several occasions the residents of the ghetto had been used for propaganda films, as can be seen in the 2010 documentary *A Film Unfinished*, which includes historical footage and reenacted scenes, so that the viewer cannot tell which are which, and does not understand for whom and what these shots were taken, being forced to look at the people in the ghetto through the bewildered eye of a Wehrmacht cameraman who himself does not know what he is filming for.

There was a dark room with videos playing. I had cold hands still. Kozyra had sneaked into a men's sauna with a fake beard, draped with towels; she looked like a dainty young man. I was still in my war, freezing as I observed her watching the sweating men, these others, for whom she was one of the guys; she belonged, as they saw it, yet she had achieved that only by camouflaging herself, by deception. Victoriously, she strolled about in the men's locker room on the long table as if on a podium, with towels around her chest and hips, until all of a sudden, she dropped one and they saw her tacked-on penis. I was shocked; she was triumphant.

I didn't know what to make of that after my walk through the ghetto, in my longing for the others. You wanted to play, but not war and peace; you wanted to play a game where you got to be someone else. She had already changed her gender, so I went behind the black curtain with the word "Casting" in big letters, and wound up in a room with papers to sign that certified my voluntary participation in the casting and willingness to answer the questions I would be asked, plus the data privacy note.

I was led into a room with dozens of hats, sunglasses, and makeup kits. I put on a red hat and a pair of sunglasses, found a lipstick I wanted on the spot, and stared at myself in the mirror. This is the way I had always wanted to be, bold and unattainable, even to myself. Then the casting began. I was asked questions, for example how I feel in the sauna among men, even though I've never been in a men's sauna, not even a mixed one, although I always feel as though I'm in a men's sauna, camouflaged by my use of the German language; everyone thinks I belong even though I'm not from here. My answers were awkward and inappropriate. The cameraman, who knew exactly what he had to do, and for whom and why, was annoyed, and I began to understand that I was supposed to play Katarzyna and answer the questions as Katarzyna. Again I was unable to slip into the role of another.

I went into the makeup room and held the lipstick in my hand, my treasure trove in this game, a joker. Never in my life had I had something that suited me so well, beguiled as I was by the light or the darkness, and I thought that one finds something of this kind only when stepping into an unfamiliar role. The lipstick was an invitation to act. I pocketed it several times, then took it out again, I wanted to take it with me but was not brave enough for theft and had the choice either to remain true to myself—that is, not to steal—or to step outside my tracks, taking action and stealing this lipstick because I coveted it and no one else did; here it was just a prop. But I couldn't do it, and feeling that I had lost in this game as well, I placed the lipstick back on the table.

at night i couldn't sleep, i dreamed of the sauna, of the ghetto, of naked bodies, contorted in death or in pleasure, i dreamed of difference, men and women, mixed, i had a fever, i told katarzyna that my name is also katerina, i quivered, i could also be a pole, i said to her, *la double vie*, how cold it is here, no acting needed, i could be anyone, but better not, never would i do it, no, better do nothing, i have also hidden away among others, or no, it was more like showing off, *show*, i didn't say shoah, you said shoah, you or i, either or, i don't know whether i ever was among my own and who are they, my own, these ruins around us and within us, and the change of language i'm undertaking to inhabit both sides, to experience i and not-i at the same time, what a thing to aspire to, i am different, but i'm not hiding, warm, and otherwise i'm shy, show, shoah, cold, quite cold all over again, but i can play the part, and i and i and i, what a strange phrase, sounds like phase, what kind of phase, as though I belonged to someone, to a family, to a language, and sometimes it even looks as though that's the case, i can't hide, and it's all in german, this language, my tacked-on gender, in german the word language is feminine and in russian it's masculine, what did I do with this switch? i can tack it onto myself, like you, katarzyna, i can get up onto the table and demonstrate it, look, everyone, i've got it! down here, o my german! i'm sweating, with my german language tacked onto my tongue

Life Records

Names, dates, three places: of birth, war, death, nothing more. The screen is displaying the death records of Zygmunt Krzewin and his wife, Hela Krzewina-Hammer. Kalisz-Warsaw-Lublin, Kalisz-Warsaw-Treblinka. The two of them were the last of our Polish branch of the family that my family in Kiev could still somewhat recall.

The finality of the word *death*, this broken record of death records, so took over my mind that I overlooked the word *testimony*. If Yad Vashem had a record of death, a document, then someone also had to have survived, someone knew what had happened and had testified to names, dates, and places. It had taken me months to lower my gaze from the death records up top in the document to a record of life down at the bottom. There I found a name, an address, and the word "niece." Mira

Kimmelman, Oak Ridge, TN, USA 1992. I couldn't count on this woman still being alive, but when I entered Mira Kimmelman Oak Ridge into the computer, a huge wave of hits came at me, Mira, a Holocaust survivor, known far beyond Tennessee, and if she was indeed still alive, she was eighty-seven years old. Mira—the niece of Hela Krzewina, who had come to Kiev back then with her husband. Mira evidently didn't know my great-grandparents, Zygmunt's parents; their spot in the death records is blank.

It was nighttime in Berlin, but it was still the middle of the day in Oak Ridge when Google provided me texts and dates of her talks, along with book offers and an interview with Mira on oakridge.com on May 5, 2009. Late at night, I sent the journalist an e-mail in the rash hope that she could contact Mira, please let her be alive, today's my birthday, though only in Berlin, in Oak Ridge it's still yesterday, two hours ago there was no such person as Mira, and in no time came the reply from the journalist, although it seemed as though I had yet to send off my message *Mira Kimmelman—my relative*. The journalist was as excited as I, because she had received a message dated tomorrow from an era far back in the past, and she promised to go straight to Mira, who didn't have a computer, with this news of the kinship, as she called it. Oak Ridge, Oak Ridge, I repeated, the call of a nocturnal bird, the world's first atomic reactor had been built here. In 1943, when the ghettos were being liquidated in Eastern Europe, the city of Oak Ridge was set up as a closed-off development to work on the Manhattan Project. The Oak Ridge National Laboratory website proudly proclaimed that it "produced plutonium for the atomic bomb that ended World War II." Oak Ridge had saved the world.

In my attempt to grasp the inner connections of my family—our leitmotifs—I spent hours reading about the Oak Ridge nuclear reactor, and just when I was thinking that you can't really live next to a reactor, I came across the date. The Oak Ridge graphite reactor was put into operation on November 4, 1943. We had learned that date in school; it marked the beginning of the battle for the liberation of Kiev, my hometown. Stalin wanted Soviet troops to march through the city on November 7, the anniversary of the revolution, and our teachers wanted us to remember it, as I did while awaiting word from Mira.

The next morning I found her reply in my mailbox, typed by the journalist. Mira was overjoyed. She was not expecting to hear from relatives, far from it, but the fewer who remained, the closer they grew. She asked me questions about my family, about myself, recommended her two books to me, particularly *Life Beyond the Holocaust*, and told me about my cousins in England. She asked me which language I preferred, English or German, and here I'd been afraid that my Berlin address might present a problem. *Beyond* stuck in my head, an apocalyptic word, Beyond Good and Evil. At the end of the e-mail was her telephone number. But I was too excited, it was like falling in love, and did not call.

I lost no time in ordering Mira's books from Amazon; *4 to 6 weeks for delivery* and *do not reply to this e-mail; this message was automatically generated*. I wrote to the ordering address, *ships from the UK*, to the distribution centers in England and America, and to some warehouses with numbers that promised to deliver the books in four to six weeks. I made it clear to them why I had to have the books by Mira right away, explained to the machines what it means to survive the Holocaust and to be found more than seventy years later, by me, Mira's relative and a loyal customer of Amazon, and that this was one of those rare instances in which time was everything. My strategy worked. A man named Hadin Abdelfattah replied on the spot, promising to do everything in his power to help me, but it really couldn't take any less than three days, sorry. I pictured him—an Egyptian?—walking through the endless rows of containers on the London docks at dusk, flashlight in hand, to find *Life Beyond the Holocaust* for me. I sensed the power of Mira, who had escaped an anonymous death and was now bringing human voices back from anonymity. To be honest, I had counted on it.

In the Internet I saw that only two members of Mira's immediate family had survived, she and her father, Moritz. After the war they moved to America. They were already living in Oak Ridge when Moritz, with the resolute handwriting of a successful Danzig merchant, wrote twenty testimonies for Yad Vashem, for his son, his wife, his parents, his siblings and their children. Benno, Shlomo, Sara, Rozka, Leon, Celina, David, Genia, Joseph, Gucia, Aron, Esther, Efraim, Maryla, Hella, Roma, Tillie. I read the records of these relatives, which I had found on the Internet seventy years after their death and instantly lost again, and decided to call Mira on Monday.

Related Through Adam

On Sunday evening the telephone rang. It was Viktor Rashkovsky, an old friend of my father's, who had never called me up. Nothing surprised me by this point. Viktor, like my father, was associated with dissident circles in Moscow. In the early 1970s Viktor immigrated to the United States and wound up somewhere in the boondocks. Although he had been a sociologist of film, he now became a Reform rabbi. Once I ran into him in Berlin on the occasion of a private recital. After someone played Schubert, there was conversation in many languages: Italian, German, Hebrew, Russian, English, Polish. I was talking about Kiev when suddenly an old man jumped up and demanded to know my full name. When I told him, he responded: Then you're Miron's daughter! Thirty-five years after emigrating from Moscow, Viktor Rashkovsky had recognized me in a city that was new to us both, even though he hadn't been thinking about me, and had never seen me. All he had to go on was the word *Kiev* and a resemblance I unknowingly bore to my parents. Not bad for a rabbi, I thought.

That was five years ago, and now he was calling me. Do you know, Katja, why I'm calling you? he asked me, and I knew the answer immediately, but my knowing struck me as absurd. He said, I've been going to the members of the congregation to visit the elderly, as I always do, and one lady, who is very much admired here, told me she had found a relative from Berlin, and she showed me a letter. I started reading about a Polish-Russian family, and then I saw your name—Katja!

The only rabbi I knew was the rabbi of the only surviving member of the Polish branch of our family. Viktor had no explanation either, and Mira had no need for one. Then they both called me up, Viktor and Mira. First Viktor spoke. I briefly contemplated the paradox of their names, as though victory (Viktor) and peace (Mir, in Russian) were calling me up at the same time, but then Mira started speaking German with me. It took my breath away. Not only did she speak better High German than I, but it was prewar German, slow and refined, with the pauses of the old-time actors; it was as though you could hear the crackling of a gramophone or of celluloid. Not a hint of Yiddish, no Polish accent. German was Mira's native language. She was from Zoppot, near Danzig, had grown up in Danzig, and was four years older than Günter Grass. She had attended a German high school there as long as she was allowed to. Afterward she went to a Polish school; she could not speak Polish very well back then.

But I'm not a blood relative of yours at all, Mira suddenly excused herself, maybe you'll find the other story more interesting. There is a blood relative of yours who survived the war, Mira said, Gutek Krzewin, Gustav, the only child of Zygmunt and Hela. When his mother was taken from the Warsaw ghetto, a Polish friend of the family had gotten him Aryan documents, and he was able to save himself in the guise of Tadeusz Podkulecki. During the war he came to Graz as a young Polish worker who loved cars, and later he was able to get a job at Opel in Vienna; eventually he even made it to Berlin, where he built bridges and streets for the Todt Organization. At the end of the war he fled to Italy, joined the British army, went to England, and was taken in by a Catholic family. He didn't tell anyone about his previous name, about the ghetto, or about his parents. His name was now Anthony Gorbutt.

These Gorbutts are your relatives, Mira said; they live in London.

I had expected Mira to tell me about the past, about Zygmunt and Hela, about their parents, but instead she told me about my new relatives and got me looking into the future. She told me about Karen and Sarah, the two English daughters of Tony Gorbutt, aka Gutek Krzewin, and their total of four children, who all lived in London, and she told me about Simon, a son of Tony who was born later. My cousins Karen and Sarah were unwittingly carrying on the family tradition of the Krzewins; they had become teachers, like many of us for generations. Then she told me about Didi, with three more children, and Didi's father, Mietek, in Israel, and at some point I couldn't follow Mira anymore. She kept on taking off in new directions, this one with that one, where they lived and how they were connected to one another and to me. Never had I been interested in such distant relatives—are we really coming together?

Tony Gorbutt died in the mid-1980s. Why had he adopted such an obviously foreign name? Was it the name of his Polish savior? The name of a friend who had died in the war? After a long search, Mira had found Gutek in England in the 1960s. He had been trained as an optical technician, then worked for a kosher catering company, and later at nightclubs.

He was a very handsome man, Mira said, and put his looks to good use in his work. He got the name Anthony Gorbutt out of the telephone book. His name was a matter of chance.

Mira couldn't hear well. I had to shout, so I found myself shouting from my apartment in Berlin all the way over to Oak Ridge, my questions about Zygmunt, my grandmother's half brother, Hela, Warsaw, Kalisz, *Life Beyond the Holocaust*, and then I locked myself in the bathroom and thought about whether the neighbors in my building in Berlin, where you could hear what was going on in everyone's apartment, were able to follow my questions. Yes, Mira had known Zygmunt personally. He was a typographer and printed the movie tickets for all five movie theaters in Kalisz, and in the summer, when Mira was at her grandparents' home in Kalisz, she watched as many movies as she could, because Zygmunt got tickets for free. Mira also knew that Zygmunt and Hela had been in Kiev to visit relatives—or was Mira just repeating what I'd told her? We were both so eager to have everything add up. Katja, you really must come to the wedding in Malaga, Mira said. Simon, Gutek's youngest son, is getting married in May. And so I have a new family, related through Adam, so to speak, with a thousand degrees of separation.

People claim it is a mixture of the will to live, random chance, and luck, but in what proportion? Mira is not embittered, not crushed. She got married, had two sons, worked, and taught. If there were a contest in this arena, Mira would hold the record in survival. She feels that she owed her survival to a small tin canteen her father entrusted to her. I promised my father I would save it, she said. From one camp to the next, where it was virtually impossible to hide even a needle, she had managed to save this tin canteen with family photos and papers; later she illustrated her book with them. In the end, it was less a matter of her saving the tin canteen than of the tin canteen saving her.

I took a look at the map. Mira's path through the war, her route through Europe, appeared beautiful. She traveled a curved route, like a city wall of the kind you might find in Lucca or Dubrovnik.

The stations of her journey were Danzig, Warsaw, Tomaszów Mazowiecki and Bliżyn-Majdanek, Auschwitz-Birkenau, Hindenburg, Gleiwitz, Mittelbau-Dora, Bergen-Belsen. A ghetto, five concentration camps, and a death march. How often might she have died? When the Warsaw ghetto was not yet closed off, but all Jews already had to wear an armband with the Jewish star, she had taken off her armband and gotten into a train leaving Warsaw. The train was policed several times, but she was not asked for her papers, which would have resulted in her death. In the Tomaszów Mazowiecki ghetto she left the hospital prematurely, out of sheer stubbornness; shortly afterward all the patients and doctors were killed. Then she was lucky enough to be brought to a work camp at the outset, and not right to Treblinka. Glasses off, someone whispered in Auschwitz, when all the nearsighted people were being sent to the gas chamber. Then she pretended to be a secretary without ever having used a typewriter. In the Hindenburg concentration camp, a satellite camp of Auschwitz, she survived typhus, with friends in the kitchen getting her extra portions of food. When she was worn out and ill, SS supervisors wrote down her number. Everyone knew what that meant, yet she was not taken away. She figured it was because the camp commander, Adolf Taube, who was known as the Angel of Death, covered for her. She also survived a ten-day death march in temperatures of minus 30 degrees Celsius and without food, and even if it might not have been exactly ten days and minus 30 degrees, what difference does that make? An old SS man had given her his extra pair of boots. In Hindenburg the prisoners put on plays, and she recited the poem "Der Erlkönig." Mira and Imre Kertész, a prisoner in Buchenwald, may have been the

zhevo in Russian, I was looking for my Krzewins, and they, too, had been woven from this linguistic ornament. Why did my great-grandfather Ozjel leave his son Zygmunt in Poland when he moved to Kiev with his family? I made my way through the marsh and the lace veils.

On the Internet I had come across Hila, who was well acquainted with the city's past, a historian, I thought, an official representative of Jewish history. But she owned a real estate company in the center of the city and managed the vanished history as her calling. Hila knew what I was looking for better than I did. I was not the first person she had helped; before me Canadians, Americans, Israelis in search of their ancestors had gone to Hila. In the archive we found the document of Ozjel Krzewin and Estera Patt's 1895 marriage, and to my astonishment it was written in calligraphic Russian. It seemed like a scene straight out of a community theater production. The dramatis personae were as follows:

Hadassa Krzewina, Ozjel Krzewin's mother, illiterate
Ozjel Krzewin, the bridegroom, son of Hadassa, father unknown, twenty years old
Estera Patt, the bride, deaf-mute, and a minor
Zelig and Chaya Patt, Estera's parents
Juda Wolfovich Erdberg, the best man
A notary named Sikorsky
The rabbi

They communicated effortlessly using sign language, the Russian clerk recorded on the marriage certificate; I noted down: father unknown, mother illiterate, bride deaf-mute.

But you're not going to talk about that in your book, my mother said when I told her. I thought she was taken aback by the word *illiterate*, because she always thought that since Adam and Eve we had been erudite and preordained to educate others, but what actually infuriated her was "father unknown"; he had his school and his profession from his father, she said, and if he never spoke of being an illegitimate child, it goes against his honor for you to do so, and you don't gain any honor from talking about it. Maybe it was a special love about which we know nothing.

I found only documents, however, and when I saw the entry "Ad. Krzewin" in the 1931 Kalisz account book, I thought: an Adam, how nice, my mother will be pleased. I in any case was pleased that this name seemed to be offering a glimpse of paradise. We are all related through Adam. Ad. Krzewin, owner of the Polonia Print Shop. I knew from Mira that Zygmunt had also worked as a typographer for quite some time. Typography was a common profession among deaf-mutes and their families, my mother once told me, because they didn't hear the blare of the machines; they focused on the visuals and on typesetting the letters, row by row, and creating the text. In the office of civil records, the clerk opened a folio. Adolf! she blurted out, Adolf Krzewin, born in 1899, died in 1938, the son of Ozjel and Estera. There's an Adolf among my Jews, *related through Adolf*, that's the last thing I would have expected. He was Zygmunt's brother, and no one knew about him. Had they worked together at the print shop? Was Adolf deaf-mute?

I had been told that their mother, Estera Patt, who was deaf-mute, had died back at the beginning of the century; then Ozjel married Anna Levi, and my grandmother Rosa came into this world. I held Estera's registration card in my hand, with all the addresses; she had often moved.

1931: Targowa, 9

1931: Brzezina

1932: Margowiska

1933: Piaskowa 7

So Estera had not died early; she had lived one year longer than Ozjel, who died in Kiev in 1939. It was now clear that Zygmunt, my great-grandfather's first son, had remained in Poland with his mother, Estera, as had Adolf, and I read the rest of Estera's addresses:

1935: Winiary

1935: res. Piłsudskriego, 35

1936: Stawiszyńska, 13

1938: Stawiszyńska, 13

The last line is in German:

28/1 1940: Reloc. to parts unknown

It was still drizzling. I took pictures of the buildings in the rain. We had jotted down a long list of addresses of who had lived where, including the address of a lace factory that had belonged to someone in my family and had been destroyed during World War I. I wasn't out to find anything specific here; the point was to search, at stake was a spiritual restitution, I couldn't see clearly, it was drizzling, and I photographed the drizzle to take something from Kalisz with me.

Hila unlocked the gate to the Jewish cemetery. The few remaining graves jutted out of the earth like weeds. She showed me the grave of the rabbi in Kalisz who had joined Zygmunt Krzewin and Hella Hammer in marriage. The grass was wet, I was cold, I wanted to get away from there, but Hila said, You have a grave in Kalisz as well, Adolf's grave, it has not been preserved, but she said it as though all you needed was to know that it had once been there, and that would make it yours.

We scoured the Internet for every Krzewin in Poland and found a Roman Catholic Kunigunda in Kalisz, and although she could not be part of our extended family, we passed by her building, which had a lingerie shop on the ground floor. Then we found a Hary Krzewin: one of us. He died as an infant. My astonishment at his existence weighed more heavily on me than the brevity of his life; I thought of him, of Adolf, of Kunigunde (a variant spelling of our Kunigunda), who had nothing to do with us, and of calling a novel *Adolf, Hary, and Kunigunde*, but I lacked the material to write it.

The past betrayed my expectations, slipping out of my grasp and committing one faux pas after another. My progenitor, who told the glorious history of my family, was an illegitimate child, but I was not supposed to write that, moreover Ozjel was not widowed early in life, and then there was this Adolf, which was a common name back then, but for me an alarming one. Adolf confirmed my fear that I had no power over the past, it lives as it pleases, and just does not manage to die.

Lost Letters

The deaf-mutes disappeared through the General Staff Arch and kept spinning their yarn, but far more calmly, as if their hands were sending off carrier pigeons every which way.

—OSIP MANDELSTAM

The history of the Krzewins did not form a taut thread; it circled and circled and got torn away like Kalisz lace. I didn't see an ornament, only little scraps, illegitimate children, names I'd never heard, lost threads, gratuitous details. I needed to spin my yarn, but I wasn't skilled at handicrafts. At this moment I was sent reinforcement in the form of Pani Ania. Not only was she in love with the town of Kalisz, but quite unusually right there in Poland, she also loved Nicholas II, the last czar of Russia. She showed me the most beautiful *kościoły* in the city, the relics of Saint Ursula; I definitely wanted to see King Casimir's chalice, but when I expressed my admiration for Catholicism, Pani Ania explained to me in refined English that she was a practicing Muslim and had studied in London for four years, and now she was working in the Kalisz prison. She was a perfect Other, a stranger, yet akin to me, and I thought, with people like that, Poland is truly not lost. It was Pani Ania who showed me the Jewish letters in the pavement of Kalisz.

People were moving along at a rapid clip. It was still drizzling, and no one seemed to be aware that some streets in the city were paved with gravestones from the old Jewish cemetery. During the war, when there were no more Jews in Kalisz, the *matzevot*, the Jewish gravestones, were removed from the cemetery, sawed into squares, and placed on the street, their backs facing upward so that the Hebrew letters could not be seen when they were stepped on. It was a system of annihilation with multiple failsafe switches. Wittingly or unwittingly, everyone who walks down the streets of Kalisz is treading on gravestones.

A few years ago, new pipelines were installed in the city, and the stones were removed and relaid, but this time no one was watching out. Some stones were reversed, and the Hebrew letters surfaced. Pani Ania showed me a few, and I tried to find others. I had to wait for the cars to go by, because the letters appeared only on the roadway.

I discovered two or three, then nothing for twenty meters, then another lettered stone, then three meters farther a few more, a game of chance with no set rules and open to everyone, a game of Memory for adults, but no one was joining in, because no one saw these letters. I was so fixated on my letters that I didn't hear the cars honking, only a song in my head, humming *Any time you feel the pain, hey Jude, refrain.* I went from house to house, from stone to stone. Someone connected to me had lived here, and a movie theater, a print shop, a letter, again drizzling, I added another letter to my collection, then another one, and yet another. I was undertaking a dubious restitution of vanished things, which I could neither appropriate nor interpret; even the standard profes-

sion of the deaf-mute, typographer, the man of letters—if it ever *was* the standard profession—no longer existed.

But I did not want the people strolling through the city to succumb to grief, on this invisible cemetery of their neighbors, strangers who were no longer there. I did not want the residents of Kalisz, when they withdrew money from the bank on the spot where the synagogue once stood, to think of these dead strangers, as though they were paying interest on their own lives.

As dusk approached and the letters disappeared, I remembered a dream I'd had as a child. The dream came like a stranger in the night; I was frightened and knew that I was being assigned a task I couldn't accomplish, and I hoped the messenger had mixed up the address.

It was dark, a church hovering over the city up on the hill, and Saint Andrew spoke, exactly as the legend tells us, and declared that a city would be built here. In the dream I had the feeling that it was not a dream, because this city named Kiev actually *was* built, and that's where I was born.

It was one of the most beautiful streets in Kiev. I walked down the steep street by myself, sensing the hovering church on my back, two figures accompanying me and silently showing me the way—I wandered lost, they knew—and snow lay on everything. My companions said, Go that way, it's all written there, and I trod through the snow. The route was unexpectedly long, and I sank deep into the snow. At the spot where the hill rose and the rear wall of a building that no longer existed ought to have been, there was a pedestal, and snow lay over it as well. I knew that there was supposed to be a book here and went to the plinth, which was about the height of a music stand, and sure enough, the book was right in front of me. My heart almost leaped out of my chest, *now! now!* However, the thing that had once been a book, or should have been one, was now an ice floe; it suddenly grew light, and I realized I'd come too late. The knowledge was gone, and it was not in my power to get it back. I was too late, by virtue of my birth and in every other way. It was not about guilt, it was just too late. And then I saw, in this porous block of ice, an earthen letter almost dissolved in the snow, a thin blade of grass jutting out of it. I tried to read the letter, but I didn't even understand what sort of alphabet it was from.

CHAPTER 4

IN THE WORLD OF UNSTRUCTURED MATTER

House Search

"I don't know that law," said K.
"All the worse for you," said the guard.
—FRANZ KAFKA

On May 8, 1932, at about noon, when my father came into this world, GPU secret service agents were standing all around him like the shepherds around the manger. The appearance of the infant was the direct result of an apartment search in Odessa, the premature birth the sign of an assassination that had occurred two months earlier.

On March 5, 1932, my great-uncle Judas Stern shot the German embassy counselor Fritz von Twardowski in the middle of Moscow. Twardowski was wounded, and Stern was arrested on the spot.

Stern had spent a long time waiting at the corner of Herzen Street and Leontievsky Lane, not far from the Kremlin, and just a few yards from the Tchaikovsky Conservatory. When an embassy car with the German flag turned the corner, he shot at the car. Two bullets injured the embassy counselor's throat and hand, and three other bullets lodged in the seat cushions. When two passersby rushed toward the assassin, he shot again. One bullet grazed the wall of the Union movie theater, and another hit a horse. Judas Stern tossed away the pistol and was arrested by members of the secret police, who turned up out of nowhere, as though they'd always been on the scene.

Judas Stern was the brother of my grandfather Semion, and thus responsible not only for the assassination but also for my father's premature birth, although the birth occurred posthumously, one month after Stern's death.

It had taken some time to track down Judas's eldest brother, Semion, because even though Semion was still living in Odessa, where all of his siblings were born as well, he had a different last name. When Semion went into the underground during the revolution, he assumed the alias Semion Petrovsky, and when the Bolsheviks came to power, he did not return to his old name, Shimon Stern, but rather stayed with the new one; at least that's how we heard it. Thanks to him and the revolution, I also have this lovely long name, which comes from the lower Russian Orthodox clergy. When I found out our original family name, I knew instantly that we are really the name we now bear; the Sterns are and will remain specters, I will never be a Stern. Semion underwent a revolutionary baptism that promised the lower orders equal rights: there is neither Jew nor Greek, there is neither bound nor free, there is neither male nor female: for you are all human beings and proletarians.

Since then, Semion had been the only one of his siblings to go by the name of Petrovsky—an earthly stone, *petrus*, among heavenly Sterns, stars—and he had not heard from his somewhat eccentric brother, whose name came out of a remote past to which there is no longer any access.

When the visitors from the secret service entered Semion's

apartment in Odessa two months after the assassination and one month after Stern's execution, he wasn't there. All those present were interrogated, and each room was systematically turned upside down. My grandmother Rita, who was far along in her pregnancy, was frightened into early labor.

Van der Lubbe

Although my father owed his premature birth to his uncle Judas, he barely knew of this uncle's existence for quite a long time; it was concealed from him for his own protection and that of the whole family. Sympathizing with Judas would have aroused suspicion, but it is not known whether anyone ever sympathized with him. It was extremely dangerous to remember Judas Stern. He himself had not spent a moment thinking about the consequences of his act for the members of his family, so why should they preserve him in the family memory?

At the end of the 1950s, when my father happened to read a couple of lines about the assassination in *Geschichte der sowjetischen Diplomatie* he instantly knew that Yeguda Mironovitch Stern and his father's missing youngest brother had to be one and the same man. He asked his father, but got no reply. He asked again, and his father brushed his question aside, dodged the issue, implored his son never to ask him about his brother again, and at some point forbade him even to mention that name.

My father stubbornly defied this order, and many years

later he again probed the matter until my grandfather Semion made a brief comment about the event in question, then never said another word about his little brother's assassination.

Van der Lubbe, Semion came out with. Van der Lubbe.

I immediately understood, my father told me; he wanted to say that his little brother was not quite right in the head, like the arsonist Marinus van der Lubbe, who had set fire to the Reichstag. By mentioning Van der Lubbe, he was revealing not only that Judas Stern had been processed and sent off but that he had been exploited by people who gulled him into committing this act, then placed the blame on others. Did my grandfather understand that Judas's actions formed the first link in a long chain of events? And did he reveal more by saying "Van der Lubbe" than he was intending?

For years I asked my father whether that was really all that Grandfather Semion had said at the time, and at some point, many years later, my father thought he recalled the word *meshuggeneh*. "Van der Lubbe" and "Such a meshuggeneh," his father apparently told him back then. Still, my father no longer remembered whether his father had explained to him that Judas Stern had been a bit insane since childhood, or he had come to understand that later on his own. My father recalls his father having said—again, years later and for no apparent reason—that in every Jewish family there is one *meshuggeneh*, or even that there is no such thing as a Jewish family without a *meshuggeneh*. My grandfather had five siblings and could get away with a statement like that. I have only one brother, so is he the one, or am I?

Meshuggeneh is the only Jewish word that has remained in my family. Is insanity my last connection to Jewishness?

The Sword of Damocles

The fear that his children would have to pay for his brother's assassination made my grandfather Semion the most tight-lipped individual in the postwar era. My father didn't know exactly what line of work Semion had been in. Everything my father did know about his father, Judas Stern's brother, was that he had worked in "the organs," as the secret service was called at the time, in administration and later in the supply department. In 1937 he achieved the impossible: he left the secret service after being handed the case of his brother-in-law, his wife Rita's brother, who was the manager of a turbine factory in Kharkiv. Or had he only been summoned as a witness? The situation was hopeless. If Semion cleared his relative of any wrongdoing, he would have been declared guilty as a conspirator in a purported family plot; if he turned against him, they would have been able to say that Semion himself was so embroiled in guilt that he sacrificed his relative to wipe out his own involvement. He left the service and was spared. Was he protected by a high-ranking official? But those officials were usually eliminated along with their protégés, so there was no explanation as to why my grandfather was not executed other than pure chance. There were at least three reasons to shoot him. He was the brother of an assassin, he was the brother-in-law of an enemy of the people, and he left the secret service.

Semion was afraid for his children and of his children, and this fear hung over my gentle, peace-loving father like a sword of Damocles.

Delusions of Grandeur

July 6, 1918, when the fatal shots were fired at the German ambassador Count Mirbach, was also a Saturday.
—*Kölnische Zeitung*, MARCH 9, 1932

My great-uncle was aiming straight at the solar plexus of the era, because he, this Soviet assassin named Judas Stern, shot at a German diplomat in Moscow one week before the elections for the president of the German Reich. It was the last year before Hitler and the first year of the famine in the Soviet Union, when two countries joined together in an alliance that propelled both to a state of insanity. And then my Stern fired his weapon.

He shot as though aiming higher than the murderers of the German ambassador Count Wilhelm von Mirbach in Moscow in 1918, a long time ago, but still fresh in people's minds, because the shots led to a rupture in the relations between the two countries. World War I had also begun with an assassination.

And isn't it insane that he fired a shot at the precise moment that the aspirant National Socialism was taking a stand against Jewish Bolshevism, which, they claimed, was prevailing in the Soviet Republic? Stalin, in turn, wanted to split the German socialists from the German Communists.

We know that today, but no one is aware of my great-uncle's role.

The more I learned, the eerier it all felt. Who stood to benefit from this assassination, and in what way? Who was intending to steer the course of history, and in what direction? In 1932, relations between Germany and the Soviet Union seemed harmonious, the two countries linked by numerous accords; in one direction went machines to be used in industry, and in the other grain and wood were sent, and the Reichswehr became known as *Lehrmeister* of the Red Army, its mentor. That is how things stood. War seemed impossible; there was almost a friendship, or so it seemed, until Stern fired off his shot, after which nothing was the same anymore. It was as though this shot, which came from my family, had shattered something in the fragile constellation of the era, as though it had anticipated future catastrophes, both here and there, as though we—and I'm including myself too—were responsible for the greatest catastrophe of the twentieth century, in a manner I could grasp only in part.

In the Archive

There were so many reasons to declare Stern insane that I'm not sure he was. As an assassin, he remained forever incomprehensible to us; you don't shoot at other people! In spite of his violent end, he was not a victim. Because we deemed him insane, the issue of responsibility did not apply to him, and so we locked him away in the past.

My only option was to mine the secret service archive at

the Lubyanka in Moscow. I'd been in that monstrous building, the headquarters of the secret service, only once, in the mid-1990s, when I went to the secret service museum in the foolish hope that the secret service would do penance. Instead, I was given instructions in continuity and the succession of Cheka, GPU, NKVD, KGB, and FSB, and I was told about heroic deeds and the hard times when "we also suffered under repressions."

At that time I was unaware that my brother had also tried to get to the files of Judas Stern in the archive, and had contacted a colonel at the Lubyanka. The colonel explained to him that the only accessible cases were those in which there was a certificate of rehabilitation—in other words, that the accused was innocent. The colonel stated that this was not the case here, and declared the documents off-limits. He's guilty, without a doubt, my brother said, but picture the situation, Colonel: an unemployed Jew without a party affiliation travels to Leningrad, steals a revolver, travels back to Moscow, spends several days hanging around unnoticed at the embassy, which has more informers than staff, and shoots at a German diplomat—in Moscow, in 1932.

—Colonel, maybe there's some indication in the files as to who stood to benefit from this kind of assassination?

—The files are scant, and contain nothing of any importance. We have the postexecution photo and the two bullets.

These bullets were more than enough, my brother said to me.

Every time I thought of the Lubyanka, the prison and torture center where Judas had disappeared, I thought of organs. We always referred to this agency as *organy*. They said he worked in the internal organs; *organy* had power over people's insides, or people simply said "He works in the organs," as though there was an organism that had swallowed all of us up. Since my childhood I've been picturing *organy*: huge dark innards with people at work, and when you go inside, you're swallowed up alive, because that is the function of the *organy*. The very idea of having to go into the archive of the Lubyanka was enough to trigger a primal fear within me.

No sooner do you go into the archive and touch a piece of paper than you are working inside the *organy*; you have become part of it, you adhere to the rules, and yet you're being toyed with, you are in its power. You breathe its air, air is for everyone, and then you are infected. Every time I so much as thought I needed to go to the archive, my limbs went limp, and the inertia of inaction stopped me from moving forward, as if to forestall the warning question: Who is touching the dust of the murdered? This involuntary refusal to go would have kept me out of danger, because those who do nothing are not subject to its power; the doers of nothing cannot be evildoers.

Although visitors to the Lubyanka were not in danger, I never entered the archive of the internal organs.

You can start with this, the archivist said, and placed three thick volumes on the table for me. Here, in the former Reichsbank, the dangers were more predictable—or did I know less about them? This is where the Nazi gold vaults were located, and because the Allies sought to prevent the gold from falling into the hands of civilians, the building was one of the few in the center of Berlin not to be bombed. Later, the Central Committee of the Socialist Unity Party used this building, and today the Foreign Office has its archive here.

An unexpected heritage: three volumes about the assassination, written in German. Reports from the German embassy in Moscow, an exchange of letters and telegrams, notes from the Foreign Office, newspaper articles, translations, court records, radio broadcasts. Hundreds of documents on the assassination carried out by Judas Stern. I thought I was the first one in the family to appear in German, but now I found the name Judas Stern on every page.

I'm sitting in front of a pile of paper, almost keeling over with excitement, without knowing what to make out of this pile. I'm learning Gothic script and will now be able to read old German books. The newspaper articles from 1932 are crumbling in my hands. I may be the first ever to read this file. Yellowed scraps of paper are lying everywhere. Every day when I head home, little morsels of paper with Gothic letters from the spring of 1932 are left behind on my table.

Daß Judas Stern in das Auto des deutschen Botschafters
Schüsse mit der Absicht, einen politischen Effekt zu erzielen,
feuert hat, steht einwandfrei fest. Der Prozeß, welcher sich
dem Militärsenat des Obersten Gerichtshofes abrollte, sollte
icht erst diese Tatsache beweisen. Was man wissen wollte,
en die Beweggründe dieser Tat, ihre Ziele und die poli-
chen Kräfte, die hinter diesem Attentat stehen. Doch
rheit hat dieser Prozeß nicht gebracht. Auf der Anklagebank

Germany itself is crumbling, becoming more and more unfathomable. The scraps of paper stick to my clothes and my computer keyboard, I'm carting this year all around, spreading the wealth, shaking this golden stockpile into the air, in the middle of Berlin, in the fall, and taking it home with me. National Socialist workers line up against Communists, the film *Kuhle Wampe; or, Who Owns the World?* comes to movie theaters, women protest, political terror is on the increase. The further I read, the faster the pages fall apart. I don't want to keep on reading, I keep on reading every day. I imagine the paper falling apart altogether at the end of my reading, and the knowledge vanishing.

I read slowly, more slowly than the events unfolded, more slowly than their pressing nature would allow. The slower I am, the longer these rather unstable, yet lovely months drag on, April, May, June 1932, more and more sun, still before Hitler, before the Reichstag fire, and I don't find anything that would lead there; even though everything is already set in motion, the world still seems whole to me. When that is no longer the case, *whole* will be transformed into *Heil*, what a greeting, and this is where I read no more.

Voices

During the first days after the assassination, the whole country was appalled, because that traitor Judas Stern had wreaked havoc on Soviet peace. The investigations had just begun, but reports already filled the newspapers. Stern had an accomplice named Vasily, there was a counterrevolutionary organization that was eager for war. A chorus of hundreds was hollering the same set of slogans.

"Assassin!"
"Shots of a provocateur!"
"Political intentions!"
"Warmongers at work!"
"Terrorists from the establishment!"
"Polish imperialists aiming to unleash a war."
"Once again, France has a hand in it!"

In countless factories in the country, rallies were taking place against the provocateur and warmonger Stern, because the country wanted peace. All my attempts to extricate Judas Stern's voice are doomed to failure from the outset. The enemies have long united to provoke a war against the Soviet Union, claims the newspaper *Volkes Stimme*.

"Assassins and White Guardists!"
"International capital and saboteurs!"
"We will not tolerate this!"

"By carrying out the assassination I was aiming to cause tensions between the Soviet Union and Germany and thus worsen the international position of the Soviet Union." It is the first time I see his own words, but at his hearing, Stern states exactly what everyone is shouting. Maybe he said something else, but this is what the newspapers reported, and these words are all we have to go on.

In the German press, the name of Judas Stern keeps cropping up in discussions of Ernst Thälmann, Adolf Hitler, and Paul von Hindenburg during the German presidential elections. My relative suddenly shot to fame, albeit briefly. Might that have been his actual goal?

No one in the chorus of voices in March 1932 seemed to notice that Judas Stern was Jewish. The German embassy in Moscow did not get caught up in the Soviet warmongering hysteria and surmised that the assassination grew out of the fretfulness of a populace suffering from hunger, resulting in large part from the forced grain exports necessary to pay for imports from Germany. Stern's shot was his way of protesting this state of affairs. It was as though the staff of the German embassy, of all people, had a true appreciation for what he had done, as though they had wanted to redeem his moral standing.

Ambassador Herbert von Dirksen was concerned especially about the way Poland was being blamed in the Soviet press, and how quickly the German Communist newspapers adopted this tone of recrimination. "Piłsudski hired the assassin Stern," the *Rote Fahne* reported without a shred of evidence, and Dirksen asked German newspaper correspondents not to single out Poland as the possible source of the assassination. Yet that seems to have been the main objective of the Soviet outcry, to convince Germany that Poland was behind the assassination and the aggression came from Poland, even though it was the Soviet Union that was striving for a bracing little war among the neighbors and was equipped to wage one, in sharp contrast to Germany. This discovery unsettled me and preyed on my mind, even more than the search for my crazy Stern.

Goethe's Secret Service

The legal proceedings would have to wait; there was an anniversary to be celebrated first with great pomp and circumstance. When privy councilor Johann Wolfgang von Goethe died on March 22, 1832, no one could have imagined the political significance the memorial ceremonies on the occasion of the hundredth anniversary of his death would assume in Russia one day, with Goethe festivals, Goethe readings, Goethe contests. The secret service provided a poetic framework for the political assassination, as though Goethe's title was sanctified by the Soviet secret service, as though Goethe was the secret director of the secret service and working on behalf of Soviet-German relations. Goethe's words "Warte nur, balde ruhest du auch"—Just wait, soon you too shall rest—were heard throughout the land in one of Russia's most famous songs, in Mikhail Lermontov's translation. The land quivered and quoted. The Faustian bargain also took on an unprecedented relevance. In the nationalized economy, there was nothing left to sell but one's own soul. Anatoly Lunacharsky, the commissar of education, traveled to Weimar to represent the Soviet Union as a land of Goethe enthusiasts and to participate in the Weimar Goethe festivities, not because the Soviet people worshiped the writer Goethe but to improve the German-Soviet atmosphere after the assassination, as *Time* magazine reported. The more talk there was about Goethe, the less would be heard about Stern. "Just wait, soon you too shall rest!" says the hangman to the convict in a Soviet joke that may have started circulating during the Goethe anniversary celebrations, perhaps in a response to the case of Judas Stern.

A *Meshuggeneh*

It is insane that that's his name, I said to my father, that is the most Jewish name ever. It was an absolutely normal name, a very common one, he replied. Papa, his name was Yeguda, Yehudi, and even if his name was Judah or Judas, it does mean Jew, nothing else, and Stern to boot. Iuda is the Russian variant, and it was written as Judas in German, a fatal error, because that was the name of the one who betrayed Jesus, none other than he, maybe the secret service wanted the people to keep hearing the name Judas, Judas lives, a traitor to our politics and the way of life, but his name was Yeguda Stern; there were many Yegudas among the prophets, poets, violinists, he could have slid right in between Isaac Stern and Yehudi Menuhin. Under different circumstances, of course, in a firm tradition, devoted and true to his ancestors, Yeguda Stern would have made his mark in a different language, would have become a visionary and entered into the annals of mankind forever. Yet of course we mustn't forget the circumstances.

Papa, how does insanity set in? Imagine a biblical Judas in the 1930s walking around Moscow with a pistol in his pocket, and the next thing you know, religion is stamped out in the country. Maybe when Mikhail Bulgakov wrote about the eternal city as it was turning fervidly atheistic in the 1930s, it was only because of our Judas that he saw modern Moscow as a backdrop for the Passion of Christ, and discovered the figure of Pontius Pilate, the streets teeming with Judases, each having already betrayed someone, maybe Bulgakov even came up with his Mephisto because of the trial of Judas Stern. Stop now, my father said, calm down, keep calm, my child, this Jesus story wasn't relevant for observant Jews, and the name Judas never felt suspicious to them. But Papa, the Jews weren't together anymore or among themselves, and there was no more faith, no more learning and no more "we," our Judas was on the road to nowhere with the whole Soviet people, a red cavalry, Papa, on hobbyhorses and with crutches: *Dahin!Dahin!Geht unser Weg!* Tis there! Tis there our path goes! What did he think of his own name? How would you have felt having this name?

A Jew making an attempt on the life of a German diplomat was like a thing summoned by Goebbels and his propaganda, a perfect creation. If Stern had not existed, Goebbels would have had to invent him, as a Bolshevist golem.

Judas and Stern: Papa, whose thoughts don't go straight to the yellow star when I say this name? "Stern" is a stern reminder of a star, and calls to mind the star-headed beauty in the Russian fairy tale, and here it's a Jewish star, a Magen David, a Star of David, a Yehuda Star—Judas Stern. Just a few years later, when our hero was already dead and gone, the star was borne on sleeves in the ghettos, an idea ahead of its time, like your mother's birth pangs, Papa.

You're making some pretty bold comparisons there, my father said.

Is our Judas a symbol or a parody, a symptom or a trigger? He shoots into the darkness, and years later, the darkness shoots back.

Was he truly insane, or did the fear of the others force him into this role? Everything we know about him was related either by witnesses who were deathly afraid and did not use their own words, or by criminals who had incited him to commit this crime.

Papa, I see something you don't see: a photo of a child. Your father and all his brothers and sisters. *Wer reitet so spät?* Who rides there so late? Your father, Semion, the eldest, is holding a little boy's hand, holding on tight, he's holding little Judas with the distraught look, or Yeguda—we'll never know for sure—he's two or three years old, your father was ten, but he looks older. Did his having to hold on tight age him? I will never tell you about this photo. Yeguda's gaze says it all, as though he knew about his future, as though this future was reflected in his eyes, filled with dread and bewilderment, as though he had seen the Gorgon Medusa, and Papa, I also saw your fear for all of us in his eyes.

The Trial

The trial began on April 4, 1932. More than 150 people poured into the courtroom on the first day of the proceedings—people's commissars and senior officials, Soviet journalists and representatives from many embassies. The foreign press turned out in full force. Two men were on trial: Judas Mironovitch Stern, twenty-eight years old, former student at the ethnography department, unemployed, and his accomplice, Sergey Sergeyevitch Vasilyev, twenty-nine years old, from a wealthy family, former student at the State Finance Academy in Moscow.

Attorney general and prosecutor general Nikolai Krylenko gave a lengthy speech about the state of the modern world. The role of the crime grew with every sentence; it took the spectators' breath away, as though they were soaring higher and higher with a case so enormous and wide-ranging that being aloft was the only way to gain an overview, and as he talked on and on, it seemed as though the People's Commissariat for Justice was lifting off from the earth and then from justice itself, casting off from the burden of proof, hovering briefly over materialism, and peering down from a great height into the twists and turns of dialectics, and so it happened that the prosecutor, Nikolai Krylenko, attained the celestial role of an omnipotent witness. There, he was in his element. Then he took a well-aimed nosedive at the defendants. "We cannot regard this crime as an isolated fact. . . . A thousand threads . . . link this act to grave and highly significant problems, not only does the fate of these two people or the fate of hundreds depend on solving these problems, but the fate of millions, not only for our people, but in many other countries."

When the audience was ready to give itself over to the grandeur of the moment, Krylenko introduced a Polish counterrevolutionary organization that consisted of Vasilyev's teachers and their families. He discussed this group's alleged assassination plans, most of which had been thwarted by the GPU, which was why, he explained, the audience was hearing about them for the first time. Thanks to the work of the secret services, all their plots had been foiled.

Everyone who supposedly belonged to this organization or knew about it was dead, in line with the principle that the only good witness is a dead witness.

Proof was sorely lacking, and the prosecution moved further and further away from the assassination, burrowing into the thicket of the subversive work of the organization whose witnesses had been killed by the secret service, allegedly because they had belonged to this organization, although they had most likely been forced to confess that they belonged to an organization about which no one except the secret service knew anything. They confessed because they would otherwise have been killed on the spot, but they were killed anyway, albeit with less torture. One dubious argument led to the next dubious argument, and the more dubious the individual parts, the more plausible the whole construction appeared to be.

It proved impossible to kill off all members of this Polish terror group, Krylenko noted after his long speech about the darkest corners of this organization, which was the only reason the counterrevolution had taken root again—and now he surely raised his voice solemnly, elated at his presence and powers of persuasion: "This assassination is the proof."

The assassination served as proof of the subversive work of an organization whose existence was known only to the secret service, and the court did not even attempt to establish any connection between the Polish organization and Stern's assassination. Even though it was the only thing to have actually taken place, the assassination was consigned to the status of a side issue. Only at the end of the indictment did it enter the discussion, when Vasilyev and Stern were alleged to have conducted political conversations and developed the idea of carrying out an assassination of the German ambassador, in order to strain relations with Germany, even if that might lead to war.

Vasilyev gives brief, clear responses; he puts in a heroic appearance. His determination earns him respect from the audience. The German journalists, still in the thrall of the Goethe anniversary, call him Mephisto. Stern was my means

to an end, Vasilyev says; had it not been for Stern, I would have found someone else. Vasilyev the head, Stern the hand, Vasilyev the puppet master, Stern the marionette, Vasilyev a resolute adversary, Stern a disoriented one, according to all the newspapers in the Soviet Union, and the foreign correspondents shared this view.

Vasilyev states that he was acting in the name of a third party, which was intended to convince Krylenko and the audience that there was a counterrevolutionary organization involved, which, however, Vasilyev would not name, because he's a man who knows the meaning of honor. Vasilyev repeats Krylenko's indictment almost verbatim, as though he's been rehearsing it for quite some time, and Krylenko listens to him with respect, as though Vasilyev is a brave enemy, whose strength he is acknowledging.

While Krylenko and Vasilyev give their statements, Stern appears despondent, according to the reports; he has already signed all the confessions: Yes, he wanted to, yes, he knew Vasilyev, yes, the ambassador, yes, in order to unsettle relations, yes, war, yes, yes, yes.

When it is Judas Stern's turn to speak, in accordance with the formalities, he slowly turns to the audience, sizes up the room wearily, and states, vehemently and distinctly, I take everything back, because un-European methods were used in the course of proceedings. No one expects this, and everyone is silent for a moment: the prosecution, the judge, and Stern's co-perpetrator. Stern repudiates all the charges, disavows his earlier statements, takes back his signatures, and recants his confession.

The foreign newspapers were in a dither over this un-European method; everyone understood that it meant torture, nowhere do I find the word itself.

If the third party whose orders Vasilyev carried out was the secret service itself, it is clear why harmonious cooperation suited Krylenko's purposes. He wanted Vasilyev to come across as a strong, unrelenting foe and thus bolster the prosecution's case, he wanted Vasilyev to play the foe, one of many foes, someone the secret service had apprehended, and function as a true marionette, an instrument of the show trial. Stern had presumably also been given his task: playing an agent, as my grandfather pictured it, a hapless Van der Lubbe. But Stern was defiant, or incapable of obedience. Maybe he broke the GPU rules. Or was he acting alone?

Three Cars

During a break in the trial, deputy people's commissar for foreign affairs Krestinsky asks Gustav Hilger, the German embassy counselor, for his license plate number. Without a second thought, Hilger gives him the number. Ten minutes later Stern is asked in court which German embassy license plate numbers he knows—he names three numbers, including Hilger's.

Gustav Hilger, who was following and commenting on the trial, the official German translator at the signing of the Ribbentrop-Molotov Pact, the man who, on September 1, 1939, at 11:00 a.m., provided the official report to the Soviet government on the invasion of Poland, who stayed in Moscow until 1941 and was witness to many more trials and major crimes, wrote a memoir, *The Incompatible Allies*, that provided insight into the methods of the proceedings and the way the defendant, Judas Stern, was treated. "From my long experience in observing Soviet show trials, I can think of no other example in which the collaboration of the prosecutor, the court and a government bureau that had a stake in the outcome of the trial had taken as blatant a form as in this incident, which was prompted by a deputy commissar for foreign affairs."

Random Chance

After the break, the duel between Krylenko and Judas Stern began.

—Citizen Stern murmured *un-European*, but it is unclear what constitutes European or un-European. And why did Citizen Stern want to shoot the German ambassador?
—It was by chance. I wanted to shoot an ambassador, and I lived nearby.
—How did the bullets wind up in the car?
—By chance. I didn't follow the path of the bullets.
—And these four bullets are also random chance?

Krylenko points to photographs of the embassy car, riddled with bullets.

—Why don't you ask the bullets! I'm no artillery expert.

The 150 people laugh out loud. Stern smiles. I laugh along with everyone in the courtroom, but I get goose bumps. I recognize our family style. A joke is more important than a correct answer, the word worth more than the outcome. It's better to be a clown than to accept rules that one doesn't respect. A joke is the weapon of the powerless. Was it Stern's intention to point out the farce that was happening here right in front of everyone?

The opulent courtroom, the laughing faces. In the middle, a reticent man with a dark, scintillating gaze who speaks haltingly and whom all trial reports describe as ludicrous and unstable, the expression on his face alternating between gloomy brooding and a crooked, foolish smile. A *meshuggeneh*?

Stern states that he acted alone. He shot at the German counselor by chance; it could have been someone else. He keeps saying, You do know that the ethnography department is quite nearby, which is where I studied. Stern continues, blaming everything on chance. Yes, random chance.

If all is regulated, if all goes according to plan, if even five years of industrialization are to be completed in four, so that everything goes awry according to plan, it means that random chance is a sign; Stern wanted to shoot at someone, to send a sign.

Stern doesn't defend himself; he seeks only to defend the independence of his will, and disputes the prosecution, he disputes the dispute and loses the thread of the argument, or maybe it only seems so because of our uncertainty as to whether something that we can hear today actually happened there.

Chance, chance, Judas Stern says. Protest, protest, Van der Lubbe says one year later.

The haze is so dense that I start to doubt whether Stern fired a shot at all. And then he turns around and asks Krylenko:

—When are you sending me into the world of unstructured matter?

Maria's Tears

Stern's older sister, Maria, from Leningrad, is summoned as a witness. She makes her way through the courtroom, seeking out her brother in the wrong area, among the spectators, as though unaware of who is being prosecuted. She loses her bearings in this room. The attendees sense that a family drama will ensue. Suddenly the room falls silent. She weeps. When she finally takes her place, Krylenko hands her a glass of water. Everyone is waiting with bated breath. Sobbing, she launches into the story of her brother, his childhood and his failures. He was a perpetual loser, she explains, a poor student and a bad brother. She says he had always been a bad child.

The correspondents report about Maria's tears, the silence in the courtroom, the look on Judas's face. Stern is in the dock, looking steadfastly at his sister. Maria, still weeping, continues her testimony. He was too young for the revolution. He was a lackluster student. He had no desire to work in the factory. Judas stole the revolver from her husband. Her brother was never a friend of the Soviets. He had always wanted to go abroad, she said in tears.

I read the court transcript and find myself running out of patience. Is she weeping because she's telling the truth, or because she has to lie?

Maria lived only a short time longer than Judas, but he was not to blame for her death. Her death was an outcome of chance. She was planning to travel to America with her husband (from whom Judas Stern had stolen the gun), on behalf of the Soviet chamber of commerce, and in preparation for this trip she went in for a routine medical examination that resulted in her death. Her husband traveled to America alone, completed his assignment, and five years later was accused of being an American spy and executed. It is unknown whether the saga of Judas Stern influenced the course of events. The couple's two sons, who, for whatever reason, had the same names as my father and his brother, Miron and Vil, these doppelgängers of my father and my uncle, vanished in the nameless orphanages of the Soviet Union.

The Apron

The final witness—a foreman from Red Rosa, the largest textile factory in the country, named in honor of Rosa Luxemburg—is called to the stand. Red Rosa was Stern's last workplace.

Stern recalled every detail.

On the first day in the factory, he was told to put on a work apron. He refused, the foreman testified.

—It's filthy, full of lice, Stern said. I don't want to get typhus.
—It's not filthy, the foreman replied.
—Yes it is, and how!
—You just don't want to work.
—Yes I do, I want to work. But I don't want typhus.
—Everyone's wearing these aprons. No one's died of them.
—They're filthy nonetheless.
—If you want to work, they're clean enough.

—And the lice: do they want to work too? Stern asked, and the foreman answered: What lice? There are no lice.

The conversation starts up again from the beginning, keeps going in circles, continues yet another round, and eventually it's no longer possible to figure out who's right, Stern or the foreman, because none of us has seen this apron, the apron that precipitated Stern's downfall.

—So, are you going to put on the apron?
—Can't I work without an apron?
—Have you seen anyone around here without an apron?
—And you think no one's gotten sick?

Comrade Judge! Krylenko says: Every fact, every act, has to make some kind of sense, especially an act of the court; there has to be a modicum of rational sense behind every act and every word. He shows that everything Stern does and says makes no sense, but he doesn't want to declare him insane, launching instead into a somewhat mocking, horror-struck, unnecessarily detailed account of the dirty pockets in Stern's overcoat, as though this proof of his uncleanliness is also proof of the crime. He takes pleasure in describing the odds and ends that were found in these pockets, claiming that in doing so he is sparing the spectators, when he actually has already told them everything.

Stern smiles, then gazes straight ahead and lapses into a kind of irony, apparently uncaring that his life depends on the outcome of this trial, perhaps because the outcome is certain anyway and he is therefore freed from the necessity of worrying.

—Why, then, did you have a newspaper article about an assassination in Japan in your coat pocket? Random chance?
—I was alone; there were no accomplices.

Maybe Stern had ample reason to refuse. He couldn't go on, he couldn't put on that apron like all the others. He wasn't all the others. His whole life felt aproned in. Subordination, humiliation, filth. He neither would nor could subordinate himself, and he lacked the strength of conviction to take on other roles. They just want me to wallow in filth, dress in filth, and produce filth together with everyone else, bursting with enthusiasm and full of joy! First you put on the apron, then everything progresses on its own. A true Soviet relinquishes any vestige of sensitivity. I'm not that sort of person.

At the factory they thought I couldn't work without putting on the apron, at the university they thought I didn't want to study because you have to join the union and I didn't want to, but I'm clean, whatever they say, compared to this filthy little world. You have to do something, show us, they said to me, show what you can do, send a signal, I showed I don't agree, not with anything, I, I, I . . .

During the trial, Stern tries, every now and then, to have his say. He is deftly prevented from doing so with questions and interruptions. At some point he gives up, lapses into silence, and even forgoes any closing remarks. The judgment reiterates Krylenko's charges, as though there were no contradictions between Stern's statement and the indictment. Stern's disclaimer is ignored as though he hasn't spoken at all, as though he's not even there, as though there is no such person as Stern. Vasilyev, by contrast, moves from his firm stance and pleads guilty, and Stern also pleads guilty, because he has fired a shot, but not guilty in the way the prosecution is framing the charge.

Two days later, Stern and Vasilyev are shot dead.

Instinct for Self-Preservation

Kiev, July 14, 2013

Dear K.,

Thanks so much for the bullets. Your thoughts fly straight into the wounds (as ballistics experts say). We ought to discuss them in detail. We can also go shooting.

In this story, the simplicity of the trial is fascinating; indeed, it is a Greek tragedy in which the outcome is absolutely certain from the outset for everyone in the know.

They were all shot. The question of exactly how they were shot still torments us, maybe because we all seem to understand that there never was any hope. Yet our hero clings to belief and hope, like an insect going around and around in a glass in the delusion that it is free, oblivious to its captivity. Die now or die later; makes no difference. These unexpected outbursts from Stern and from you, his frenzy in the face of death, every hope, even if it's just your own, are what is interesting, strange, and tormenting, and this is where literature begins and history ends. What do you need this person for, why are you stirring up his ashes? And how does it feel to be connected to him?

You say that your text is the desperate attempt to establish this connection. But is that going to work? The instinct for self-preservation stays awake and watches us sharply in these minutes.

Knife blades emerge from the wall and move about, not far from the body. They hang somewhere, and sometimes they glide oh so close, and you describe them theoretically (I can't even do that), but you can't render this horror and the dreadfulness of their presence because rendering these feelings means acknowledging them and allowing them inside. That's how terrible these things are.

Yours, Z.

Forget Herostratus

The German ambassador, Herbert von Dirksen, who many believed was the intended target of the assassination, was convinced that my great-uncle had acted alone. He compared Judas Stern, whom he considered immature, unstable, and conceited, to Herostratus of Ephesus, whose quest for glory and pursuit of immortality led him to set fire to the Temple of Artemis to immortalize his name. Although any mention of his name was subsequently prohibited, historians wrote about him, and he turned into a type; even the date of the crime has been identified ever since someone noted that the night Herostratus burned down the temple was the very night when Alexander the Great was born. Judas Stern had become a type even before he had committed his crime; the newspapers wrote about him and were read by others seeking notoriety and a means of protest, maybe even by Van der Lubbe.

While these newspapers were still reporting on the deficiencies in the Soviet justice system, about "expiation without clarification," the Russian emigrant press was praising the assassin Stern: "A hero who stood alone against the Soviet power and who embodies a new Russian *intelligentsiya*." From Paris to Harbin, people were still hoping that the Bolshevik power was temporary, that one would return home at some point, that Stern was one of thousands of people who took issue with Soviet despotism and who would now go public in order to protest.

The assassination created a stir, but Stern hadn't produced heroes; still, he had let the genie out of the bottle. Paul Gorguloff, a Russian émigré in Paris, in search of justice, sparked into action by the press reports, shot French president Paul Doumer at a book fair in Paris on May 6, 1932, and fatally wounded him. All of France was shocked: the country had given shelter to immigrants, and one of them killed their president. Gorguloff was an officer without a country, a physician who was not allowed to practice medicine, and an author who published his works under a Russian pseudonym, Bred, "delirium."

The Herostratus syndrome took hold among neurotic, disaffected, unstable, and unfortunate individuals. They regarded an assassination as their last chance to win fame, to protest, to show the others; they were disenchanted and often profoundly correct in their convictions, and they took up arms.

Gorgon Medusa

He shot with intent to kill, and that makes it hard for me to understand him.

you are at their mercy, they won't kill you on the spot, each to his own pleasure, they will scientifically monitor your transition from a human being to a bundle of blood, death is the greatest grace, *they* will teach you that, not god. you hope, you supply answers, you are promised that if you say it they'll let you go back to sleep, you hope again, that they leave you alone, your body keeps you going, your body, you didn't expect it, you name these names in the brief moment you are there, all the names you know and all the places, they are part of the conspiracy because you know them, at some point the words disappear and you can only repeat what you are told, or deny everything, no more. did I kill a horse? now they can do anything with you, but they keep you at the precipice of life, in uncharted territory

even so, i'm not afraid, as though not feeling the pain of the tortured stern, yes, he fired a shot. i would die there instantly, i wouldn't offer any resistance, i would denounce all my friends if faced with un-european methods, instantly, regardless of whether we'd done something, if i name all of them they won't capture anyone, just wait, in the state of security and for the sake of security, but being tortured for a whole month, always those questions and promises, then questions and promises all over again, torture, promises, then torture, and maybe no execution after all, abandon all hope, we're not granted that, when are you sending me into the world of unstructured matter?

i know i should be afraid, i don't even want to look, i know that if you let in this fear you turn to stone as though gazing at the gorgon medusa, this fear is the medusa herself, but i have a means of protection, my shield, my name. my name has stone within it, peter, petrification, stone, thanks to a grandfather, it was worth changing our name, i will not turn to stone, and i am also not guilty, katerina the pure, immaculate, i could look at the medusa, but something holds me back, as though there was a hero with a shield between stern and me, perseus, he's holding a shield, and i see the medusa reflected in it, not directly, with refractions of fear, fear in shards, i see shards of fear, they tear away at me, there is a price to pay all over, hand over a shred of one's soul, no, at first they don't want to buy the whole soul, just parts of it, membership dues to the union, to the young party, to the proletariat, cogs, we're all cogs in a big machine, and if you have phantom pain, don't be whiny, better tell a joke, and now smile, please, just a snapshot, so to speak, so it's gentler, the transition, those who laugh live longer, *soon you too shall rest*, i'm not afraid, perseus is holding a shield in front of my eyes, a mirror image of terror, instinct for self-preservation

the grinding of the machines, aortic rupture, bones, machines that crush consciousness into powder, and now comes the second wave, hunger, the grain is taken away, part of it shipped to other countries, and they send us machines, which, if we don't know how to use them, are more useless than people who die, machines grind and grind up, everything turns to dust or to bread and goes to the devil, and there is no place left where there is no corruption or crime, and everyone has already fired a shot except me

Karl versus Judas

In the summer of 1932 Karl Albrecht, a Communist and a leading Soviet unionist, was locked up in the infamous Butyrka prison in Moscow after criticizing corruption in the timber industry. A man was placed in his cell; Albrecht, who later became a National Socialist, figured that this man was from the secret service, which was unusual, because an agent was normally not housed with the other prisoners, and this agent told him about the trial of Stern and Vasilyev. He claims that Stern and Vasilyev were GPU agents assigned the task of killing ambassador Herbert von Dirksen, but they failed miserably. The murder was supposed to force Germany into the position of issuing a war ultimatum; the union of the revolutions in both countries would have meant war, Stalin was convinced. The two of them were supposedly promised that they could go underground and, with new passports, return to freedom, but only after a trial that was conducted in an orderly manner, followed by an execution with fake ammunition, staged for the press and international observers. Afterward, agents Stern and Vasilyev would continue to work for the GPU. With this assurance, both took their places facing the wall. At the last second, Judas Stern realized that the execution was no mere orchestration. He turned to his shooter, called out *Brother! What did I . . .* , and fell over dead. The stranger reported that bloody sacks were carted off, and soon after, the stranger himself disappeared.

Wind Rose

I'm almost proud, as though my great-uncle had carried out a heroic act. Did he intend his shots to provoke a war between the Soviet Union and Germany? Or was he hoping to rescue all the ordinary people, all the sufferers? Or did he want to accomplish both, as a marionette, as an agent, as a free individual, who just randomly happened to be Judas Stern?

Thirteen years later came the day of liberation, the day of the victory over fascism—and those of us who are from over there, from the other side, will always say, the day of victory, meaning May 9. On May 8, my father had turned thirteen, and if he'd still been Jewish, he would have celebrated his bar mitzvah on this day, the religious age of majority, the day of taking on the duties of an adult, on the very eve of the victory over fascism, but he did not get to know the term bar mitzvah and its meaning until forty years later.

I always wanted to engage with history, my father told me, but never wanted history to engage with me, and he also claimed that we don't need relatives to feel a connection to history. And I said, Yes we do, I'm inclined to gather everything into a sprawling panorama, as though we ourselves were swirling within the wind rose of the events, if only because of an insane relative from whom we can't learn anything.

CHAPTER 5

BABI YAR

A Walk

–I'll say a word and you tell me what it means. Okay?

–Okay.

–Babi Yar.

–Does it have something to do with Indians?

–Not exactly.

–So what is it?

–It's a ravine near Kiev.

—*THE NAKED MAN ON THE PLAYING FIELD*
FILM BY KONRAD WOLF, 1974

I hadn't been here for a long time. Babi Yar is no longer on the outskirts of the city. Today you can take the subway to the ravine. Metropolitan Kiev has long since encompassed Babi Yar. A kiosk selling Tuborg beer, a newsstand, the monument for the murdered children. A little blue sock is lying on the pedestal. Someone must have lost it. I need oxygen. Athletic women are jogging by, boys are playing soccer, men are drinking beer on the benches, and retirees are collecting bottles—the usual urban goings-on. The apartments in the area are no cheaper than elsewhere, because Babi Yar is a park. I try to find my way. Babi Yar. *Women's ravine*. An oddly sweet name. Do you mean *baby year*? a librarian in Berlin had asked me when I requested books on the subject. No, I won't get lost here, I have several city maps with me, even one from 2006, designed for the sport of orienteering in Babi Yar.

Does a place stay the same place if, at this place, people murder, bury, blast, hollow out, burn, grind up, scatter, hold their tongues, plant, lie, create landfills and backfills, fill up with concrete, once again hold their tongues, block off, arrest mourners, and then later construct ten monuments, commemorate their own victims once a year, or think they have nothing to do with it?

Many years ago I asked David, a friend who made it a habit to go to Babi Yar on that day every year, whether he had relatives lying here. He told me that this was the stupidest question he had ever heard. Now I finally understand what he meant. It makes no difference who you are and whether you have loved ones to mourn here—or did he just want it to make no difference?—for him, it was a matter of decency. I'd like to speak about this walk as if it were possible to keep silent that also my relatives were murdered here, like a person in the abstract, a person per se, and not just as a descendant of the Jewish people to whom my only connection is the search for missing gravestones, as if it were possible to go for a walk as such a person at this odd place called Babi Yar.

Babi Yar is a part of my history, and I have no other, but I am not here on that account, or not exclusively. There is something that brings me here because I believe that there are no strangers among victims. Here, everybody has someone.

I had always thought that the Jews in the ghetto were privileged; I almost said they were lucky. They had more time to understand which way things were going and that they would probably soon face death. Ten days after the Germans entered Kiev, in late September 1941, the entire remaining Jewish population was killed here in Babi Yar, barely hidden from the eyes of the rest of the residents of the city and with the help of the Ukrainian Auxiliary Police. Kiev, the oldest Russian city in which the Jews also had been living for a thousand years, became *judenfrei*. Most people talk about these victims as Jews, often meaning simply "the others." That is misleading, for those who had to die were not the others; they were, rather, friends from school, kids next door, neighbors, grandmas and uncles, biblical elders and their Soviet grandchildren, who were last seen on September 29 on the streets of Kiev in an endless train of their own funeral procession along Bolshaya Zhitomirskaya.

I have never understood why this misfortune should always be the misfortune of the others. "All Jews in the city of Kiev and the surrounding area are to report to the corner of Melnik and Dekhtyarev Street (at the cemeteries) at 8:00 a.m. on Monday, September 29, 1941." So read the Wehrmacht posters, and the building supervisors had their books at the ready to ensure that All really did go. When they came to Babi Yar, they had to undress; naked they went through the rows of police, being shoved, shouted at, and beaten—and at the spot where the sky shone through the opening, at the edge of the ravine, they were shot to death with machine guns from both sides. Or alternatively: the naked living lay down on the naked dead, and only then did the shots ring out; the children were just thrown onto the dead, they were buried alive to save ammunition.

I am walking through a flat countryside overrun with scraggly plants. The operation had gone smoothly, the leaders of the Sonderkommando reported to Berlin in early October 1941. Did it happen here? People are out walking, chatting, gesturing with their hands in the sun. I do not hear anything. The past swallows up all the sounds of the present. Nothing more comes along. No room left for anything new. I feel as though these walkers and I are moving on different screens. Is there something in their gestures that betrays the origins of human violence? Or the tendency to become a victim? Would I prefer it if Babi Yar now looked like a moonscape? Exotic? Toxic? All people—consumed by suffering? Why don't they see what I see?

Kiev was one of many locales where it took place; it is said to be the largest two-day massacre of the Holocaust. Thirty-three thousand, seven hundred and seventy-one people were killed in two days. An oddly precise number. And later another 17,000 Jews, and later still they stopped counting. The first to be killed in Babi Yar were patients from the psychiatric institution. They were murdered very quietly at the edge of the ravine in gas vans, on the grounds of the clinic. A few days later it was the turn of the Jews. The killings went on for two years: prisoners of war, partisans, sailors in the Kiev fleet, young women, more Jews from the region, passersby who were apprehended right on the street, three complete gypsy camps, priests and Ukrainian nationalists who had first collaborated with the Germans and then also became their victims. According to various calculations, between 100,000 and 200,000 people were killed in Babi Yar. This plus or minus of 100,000—it is not even clear whether there was one Babi Yar or two.

Before there was a subway here, my parents and I came to Babi Yar from the other direction. We had a look at the frescoes in the twelfth-century St. Cyril's Church, the Last Judgment, the angel rolling up the heavens, the Art Nouveau frescoes of Mikhail Vrubel, the Madonna with her heavy-lidded eyes, and the outpouring of the Holy Spirit onto the apostles, for which the inmates from the nearby institution had served as models. With such spiritual buffering, we went through the Babi Yar ravine, and I had only a very vague notion of what sort of place this was, I didn't even know whether it had any connection to my family and what kind of life-affirming ritual, as I perceived it, we were performing here alone. Much later, my parents told me that their grandparents and the lovely Lyolya were lying here somewhere. My babushka is also in Babi Yar, my father told me, she just did not make it this far.

Eventually we got to the monument, the first and, at that time, the only monument that had been dedicated, thirty-five years after the massacre, at the wrong place and on the wrong day. Muscular Soviet heroes—a sailor, a partisan, and a Ukrainian woman—conquering the past. The words *heroism*, *courage*, *fatherland*, *daring*, bounced off me like Ping-Pong balls. Not a word about the fact that the Jews of Kiev are lying here as well.

In the summer of 1943, when the Red Army was approaching Kiev, three hundred prisoners of war in the neighboring Syrets concentration camp dug up the dead day and night, piled up stacks of twenty-five hundred corpses at a time, burned them, and ground up the bones. Dust can't be counted. The people were forced to cover up the tracks, and they too were then murdered, so that those who had seen would also be covered up, and in the end nothing remained, no trace, no people, no narrative. The prisoners of war foresaw their fate and tried to flee. Of the three hundred, no more than fourteen survived—the only witnesses.

After the war, investigations were carried out here, although there was hardly anything left to investigate, and Stalin's anti-Semitic policies put a quick end to any inquiries. Authors of books such as *The Black Book of the Russian Jewry*, who gathered the facts and wrote up reports, were persecuted, as were Jewish doctors, who were accused of preparing poisons. One of Stalin's last acts was to order the execution of the Jewish Anti-Fascist Committee. The members of this committee included some of the last authors to have written in Yiddish.

Hitler killed the readers, and Stalin the writers; that's how my father summed up the disappearance of Yiddish. Those who had survived the war were again in danger. Jews, half Jews, quarter Jews—once again, people learned to taste the percentages until their tongues froze on the cold metal. They were stigmatized as rootless cosmopolitans, maybe because they were killed irrespective of borders, they who maintained forbidden connections abroad, and therefore could never belong to the big family of the Soviet sister nations.

For a full twenty years, there was no mention of the massacres here in Babi Yar, no monument, no marker, no sign. Killing was followed by silence.

When I look for the majestic ravine today—which before the war was two and a half kilometers long, up to sixty meters deep, and quite steep—I cannot find it. For ten years a brick factory pumped its loam pulp, sand, clay, and water into the ravine; the Soviet government wanted to liquidate Babi Yar as a place as well. In 1961, however, an earth dam collapsed at Babi Yar, and a mudslide poured into the city, killing 1,500 people. That, too, was kept secret. The mud was brought back to Babi Yar and used to fill up the ravine again.

A few months later a poem by Yevgeny Yevtushenko was published in the *Literaturnaya Gazeta.*

No monument stands over Babi Yar.
A drop sheer as a crude gravestone.
I am afraid. Today I am as old in years as all the Jewish people.
Now I seem to be a Jew.

The people were shouting to one another, calling each other up on the phone, my mother told me; we were crying for joy that the catastrophe was finally being spoken about in public. A Russian poet had shown sympathy for the Jewish victims, for all of them, it seemed like a miracle. In his poem it was no longer their dead, the dead of the eternal Others, and it had been printed in the newspapers.

"I am each old man here shot dead, / I am every child here shot dead." Within a month the poem had been translated into seventy languages—the German translation was by Paul Celan—and Shostakovich set it to music in the adagio of his Symphony no. 13. It seemed as though this global calamity was no longer adrift, as though honor had been restored to the memory.

But not in Kiev. It took six more years for a small memorial stone to be placed in Babi Yar. Even then, when people came to this stone with flowers once a year, on September 29, the militia tried to prevent these "initiatives," as they were called. My friend David and many others emigrated from Kiev, not only because life was being made hard for them but also because their past, their grief, their places, had been stolen from them. David once spent fifteen days in prison for having left flowers at a tree in Babi Yar; the charge was "infringing on public order and strewing garbage in a public place."

There must have been hundreds, even thousands, of people who saw the Jews as they proceeded through the city; there must have been tens of thousands who heard about it. In October the entire city knew what kind of "resettlement" had taken place, particularly once the clothes and valuables of the murder victims had been distributed to the German army. In November 1943, when Kiev was liberated, only a fifth of the population was left in the city. Some were at the front, many had fled into the depths of the countryside, and a large percentage had been murdered or deported to Germany. Who was there to tell about Babi Yar, and to whom?

Anatoly Kuznetsov grew up near the ravine. He was eleven years old when the executions took place in the immediate vicinity of his home. After the war he studied ballet and danced in the Kiev Opera, but he could not get Babi Yar out of his mind; he could not stand the silence. He spent years compiling all the traces he could find of what had happened, and questioning witnesses. In 1966 he published the first book about Babi Yar, and he guided many people through the ravine, including the poet Yevgeny Yevtushenko, to show that there was nothing more to show—only to tell.

I go from monument to monument. Grandmothers look at them as they walk around with their grandchildren, often simply because they see me doing it. Twenty years ago, when Ukraine became independent, all groups of victims began to get monuments: a wooden cross for the Ukrainian nationalists, a memorial for the forced laborers from the East, one for two members of the clergy who joined the resistance, a plaque for the gypsies. Ten monuments, but no shared memory; even in commemoration, there was no end to *selection*.

What I am missing is the word *human*. Who do these victims belong to? Are they orphans of our failed memory? Or are they all ours? On the hill, like a charred tree, there is a menorah, the first Jewish monument for Babi Yar, dedicated fifty years after the event. I am really unsettled by a plaque that was mounted in the late 1980s so that the heroism and daring of the Soviet people would also be recognized in Yiddish. How many people in this city might still be able to read Yiddish? Twenty? Do languages disappear by themselves? Or is the plaque appealing directly to God?

In one of Kiev's large synagogues there was a state-run puppet theater after the war. One of the puppeteers was Dina Pronicheva, who had managed to escape from the ravine on September 29, 1941, and later appeared as a witness in many trials. I think how the final chapter of this metamorphosis is a puppet theater in a synagogue employing a survivor of Babi Yar.

I continue walking past the monuments in the direction of St. Cyril's Church. I climb the hill, the shrubbery gets wilder, the people disappear, the main-street traffic noise can no longer be heard. On the left a densely overgrown escarpment comes into view, and I see three graves with metal crosses. The unauthorized graves of Babi Yar. One says, "Here, too, human beings were shot in 1941. Let their souls rest in peace!"

Never have I seen a grave with the inscription "Here, too." Now I have arrived in Babi Yar. I'm standing in the woods, and a funeral wreath is hanging up in a tree. Who brought it here? Are wreaths growing from the trees here? Should Babi Yar be left to run to seed? Given over to animals and plants?

Suddenly a bright metallic sound pierces the air, and a surprising view opens up before my eyes. Dozens of young men in heavy, richly adorned garments are acting out Tolkien's *Lord of the Rings* in a glade with gleaming golden foliage. No path leads here. I ask the Lord of the Rings how to get out of the woods, toward the church, and he says, Angel will help you. Angel is the name of the boy who walks with me. We sink to our knees in leaves, see a few overgrown gravestones with Russian or Hebrew inscriptions. At some point there were cemeteries here, the old Jewish cemetery, the Russian soldiers' cemetery, and the Karaite Jewish Cemetery; they were demolished after the war, and today there are a TV tower and a TV studio on one part of the vast expanse. A few graves are still scattered about, the gravestones peeping out of the earth like mushrooms undergoing an inner process of growth. We are walking on a path that has been closed off, and it feels as though we are engaged in something forbidden, moving against the course of time, in the direction of the psychiatric clinic and toward the church in which an angel rolls out the heavens, and when I guardedly ask my Angel where we are, he says, This was once Babi Yar.

Riva, Rita, Margarita

When I was small, my grandmother Margarita, my father's mother, whom we called Rita although she was originally named Rebecca, Riva for short, went out onto the balcony of our seventh-floor apartment in Kiev, gazed into the distance, beyond the trees, across the canal over to the man-made island with its prefabricated buildings, and screamed, Help! The fascists want to kill me! The older she got, the more fascists there were, and eventually everyone around her was a fascist; she was besieged by her closest relatives, and we had also become fascists.

I didn't want to talk about her, since I didn't experience her lucid moments, and with every look in her direction I sensed that I was lifting up a veil that was better kept down, because a dark, torpid madness, the most intimate of all things, was dwelling there. Out of consideration for the others, who have held their tongues, I cannot tell the story of how agonizingly she died, clinging to her hated life, when I was seven years old.

When my father talked about his mother, he said that she had beautiful dark blond hair, styled in large waves, and yes, uncommonly beautiful, he repeated, you know, she had one wave that swept across her head, contrary to all thoughts—and he ran his hand over his own hair, where he had a similar wave. He always took pains to say something kind about her, and he did say kind things, which was wonderful, but I sensed his effort, and how hard it was for him to talk about her.

In the early 1920s, when Rita lived in Kharkov and had her whole life ahead of her, she wanted to join the Party. She had gotten a recommendation from her neighbor, Vyacheslav Molotov. For a brief time they lived next door to each other on the same floor, but at that time no one could have guessed that Molotov would become famous throughout the world, along with Ribbentrop and their pact. By contrast, nothing is known about my grandmother; she left neither historical traces nor great deeds for posterity, nothing except us. Her obscurity and her insanity affect me more than his partition of Europe and the dazzling ring of his name.

Rita had taught children in vocational schools on and off, mostly ideological subjects. She was strict and unjust, my father once said, and I know that her injustice and her power over the students pained him, because one wants to love one's own mother, and for him that was no easy matter. She was anxious, fretful, and sickly, and I knew that she'd always been anxious, fretful, and sickly, both before and after the war.

Maybe Rita's madness was triggered by something she had seen as a child, as I'd been told. Her brother was killed as an infant, in the 1905 Pogrom of Odessa, his head smashed against the wall. She was seven years old and is said to have witnessed this. No one knows why she survived; maybe she was allowed to live with the fleeting notion that the most important thing was not death but power over the human soul. I don't know who told me this story, nor do I know whether it's true, because I can't imagine that happening, but if someone did tell me this story, it could only be my father, yet I am even less able to imagine him telling it, so as time went on, I never dared to ask him, to torment him with a repetition of the story, with the death of the child. This story set me aquiver, but in so hazy a manner that it appeared to arise from the interplay of a feeble imagination and a weak memory. Yet what better proof can there be of the historical veracity of this incident?

But back then, when I was not even seven years old and knew nothing about Rebecca or Riva, only about my grandmother Rita, Margarita, I didn't include her name in the deep dark past, but in my own little world. For me, she was Rita, Margarita, Margaritka, a flower, a daisy, and they grew everywhere.

Anna and Lyolya

When my great-grandmother Anna and my great-aunt Lyolya walked among the crowds on Bolshaya Zhitomirskaya, their domestic help, Natasha, came with them part of the way. She could not stop crying, and Anna reprimanded Natasha for her tears: Calm down, we've always had a good relationship with the Germans. After the war, when Natasha found my grandmother Rosa, Anna's daughter, she told Rosa about Anna's final, unsettling statement.

I asked my mother why her grandmother Anna had stayed in Kiev. She didn't want to leave the grave of her husband, Ozjel, my mother said with conviction, and added with a little less certainty, Anna thought there was no need to flee, or maybe she was too old to do so, my mother said, and actually she didn't really know why.

Anna was killed in Babi Yar, although my parents never used the word *killed*. They said, Anna is lying in Babi Yar, as though this lying could confer peace on the souls of Anna and my parents, setting aside the question of the originators of the deed. They found it painful to ponder the question of originators of the deed, because they did not want to be angry at anyone, they couldn't hate anyone. For them, the events assumed mythic proportions, no longer accessible to us mere mortals, an incontestable occurrence that could not be subject to human scrutiny.

My image of Anna is woven together from a set of extraneous, unmatching threads. I only knew that Anna was born in Łódź, as the daughter of a miller, Schubert's *Die schöne Müllerin*, I thought, and I also knew that her siblings in Łódź and elsewhere worked in the textile industry and accumulated wealth. Anna, on the other hand, spent her whole life far away in Kiev, working in the huge household of Ozjel's school for the deaf and mute, teaching and helping in the workshops, always in motion, and doing everything that needed doing for the children. Even in the photograph that Natasha managed to save throughout the war, Anna was wearing an apron. The picture is not a snapshot; Anna struck a pose as though she had spruced up for the occasion, her gaze proud and commanding.

Anna knew enough not to believe her own words about a good relationship to the Germans; after all, she had sent packages to occupied Warsaw when World War II broke out and received letters from Warsaw until 1941. Whom was she trying to comfort, shame, or trick with this talk of a good relationship? My aunt Lida was thirteen years old when she saw her grandmother Anna for the last time, and she spent a good bit of her life in a similar apron. Sixty years after Anna's death, when Lida herself was old and ailing, she suddenly said, I'm going to Babushka Anna, as though she had been thinking of Anna incessantly, although she never spoke about her. Maybe Lida was wearing her apron in memoriam? Everyone was horrified by what Lida had said; it was a whiff from the beyond, and they understood that Lida was giving up, but at the same time she had made a choice, she wanted to go, just as Anna had made a choice when she stayed in Kiev. Lida did not believe in Anna's surrender to fate. Teachers of deaf-mutes cannot afford to surrender, Lida evidently claimed. Maybe she thought it was Anna's pride, the pride of a teacher who believed she could transform people, at times of war and peace, hubris, the belief that she, Anna Levi-Krzewina, might be able to prevent, if not the invasion, then at least the subsequent escalation, and be able to do so not by carrying out a heroic deed but rather by expressing her disapproval or disbelief or simply by ignoring violence. She was too proud to turn her back and flee the enemy; she stayed to demonstrate her dignity and thereby maybe teach the enemy a valuable lesson, in the evident hope that if she stayed, if she did not believe in the evil in man, especially in the evil in Germans, the Germans, too, would believe in their good relation to Anna Levi-Krzewina rather than in the evil within themselves, the idea being that if she herself believed in it or at least acted as such, they would also believe in it or act as such too, Anna and the Germans, reciprocally, you might say, because if this woman had no fear on account of her sheer dignity, they couldn't come up with grounds for fear either, because how could her opponent turn down such a generous offer? Anna had challenged the invincible German army to a duel, but the Germans did not recognize her weapon. Did pride matter more to her than survival? Or did she think that only losers can retain their honor, losers in the military sense, of course, at a time like this, when she was stripped of every shred of dignity, or did she not want to go on living, because there was no more honor to be had if this kind of thing could occur?

Lyolya, my grandmother Rosa's younger sister, lies in Babi Yar as well. Why didn't Anna convince her daughter to leave the city? Lyolya's real name was Elena, and she was called beautiful Lyolya, presumably to avoid comparisons with beautiful Helen; wars were fought for Helen, and my family had always been against that. Lyolya did not stay behind in Kiev solely because of her mother, the usual fate of the youngest child; no, she was already thirty and married, and her husband, Vladimir Grudin, many years her senior, a professor at the conservatory, a composer who issued recordings of musical renditions of Pushkin's writings and had written a ballet for *Alice in Wonderland*, this Vladimir, I was told, had had enough of the Soviet power, and he was convinced that it would be better if the Germans came. In spite of his love of Gustav Mahler, who had long since been banned from the German concert halls, he believed that things would get better under the Germans, because they simply couldn't get any worse. And Lyolya, the dreamy princess, believed him, the way many people, under one or another power, believed back then that the war would bring better times for everyday life, for work, and for music. Lyolya was a pianist, one person told me, but she also sewed, someone else said, and she even worked in a garment factory. Vladimir didn't want her to work—or is it that he didn't want her to play? They lived a comfortable life on Bolshaya Zhitomirskaya, only three houses down the street from Anna; they had no children, but they did have an immense grand piano as well as an upright, many cats, and many cushions on the sofas. Only once did I see a photograph of Lyolya, which showed her bending over the water of a narrow, sparkling river with a vague sort of movement, both graceful and awkward, and the flecks of light that played on the surface of the water, as I recall, seemed to blind not only her but also me.

Throughout my childhood, I had been afraid of the piano that had come to Kiev as war booty and wound up in our family in the 1960s. It stood in my room like an unknown object from an alien world, with an inscription, "Kaiserlicher Hoflieferant C. Hoffmann," in golden letters. With every piano lesson I sank deeper into the river of an inexplicable, rising fear, and at some point I stopped taking lessons.

At the age of seventeen I dropped a cup, and my aunt Lida, the surface of whose life had been rippled by my mishap, said, You're like Lyolya. I already knew who Lyolya was, and her remark stopped me short, so that I didn't dare to ask Lida what she had meant by saying "like Lyolya."

When the All Jews orders were posted on the walls of the city, Vladimir Grudin disappeared. He did not come home for days, and some people said that he had gone to headquarters to get a permission form for Lyolya so as to prevent her "resettlement."

My grandmother Rosa, Lyolya's sister, didn't believe that version of the story, even though she never told me she considered it a lie, but I sensed that she never forgave him. Vladimir disappeared, and showed up years later in the United States. He lived another forty years, and my grandmother Rosa even thought she had heard her brother-in-law on the radio, on Voice of America. But Lyolya waited, and she was still waiting even as she walked with her mother down Bolshaya Zhitomirskaya to the ravine. But maybe Vladimir is not to blame. Why, though, did my grandmother sometimes say "Anything but Mahler," as if begging for mercy? It was eerie how quickly she recognized Mahler as a danger, as a source of alarm, slamming shut and retreating into a shell by reflex, every time, as though Mahler was to blame for everything, as though Mahler was a sign. It was a false conclusion, standing at the end of a whole series of entrenched errors. It was an error on the part of the Germans to prohibit Mahler and not to recognize Anna's weapons, it was an error on Vladimir Grudin's part to have trusted the Germans, and it was an error on Lyolya's part to believe Vladimir that everything would be fine, and to stay and to wait.

One day in April a few years ago, Lida's daughter, Marina, called up my mother to wish her son—that is, my brother—a happy birthday, because we have a tradition of sending best wishes to the parents when their children are celebrating their birthdays, even when the children have long grown up and are living far away. After conveying her birthday wishes, she added, I'm calling you to celebrate three birthdays. My mother knew about two of them—her son and her grandson were born on the same day, funnily enough, but the third one? Lyolya, Marina said, Lyolya was also born on this day. None of us ever showed an interest in finding out the birthday of this woman who died so young. My grandmother Rosa, Lyolya's sister, never mentioned it, not even when her own daughter, my mother, gave birth to her first child on this very day. My aunt Lida never told my mother either, even though she had known about this birthday her entire life and

the gallows didn't fit with red-haired, freckle-faced, roguish Arnold. Then there was the sound of drums, or no, the hangman rolled up his sleeves, and then the sounds of drums really set in, he was told to kneel down, or no, no, he was led to his execution, it was in the war in a Ukrainian village where no one knew that he was Jewish, he had worked as a butcher and sold bad meat, or he was a cobbler, and even after repairing a shoe a nail still stuck out, or he was a revolutionary, partisan, or rebel, or Arnold was betrayed and led to his execution, more than once, as though it was possible to be executed more than once, people all in black with rifles led Arnold off, he looking like a wayward clown, how they head to the woods, that looks so grotesque, almost amusing, that it can't possibly turn out badly, and at this moment our army storms into the city and liberates it, from the Germans, from the White Army, from the outsiders, frees Arnold and frees Abrasha and frees Abram, one and the same person, my great-uncle, Rosa and Lyolya's brother, because that was his real name, Abram, Abrasha. When I was little I couldn't put my finger on which war had been raging out there, which army, the Red or the White, had stormed into the city; they always said *our* army, but I didn't understand whether it was our heroic *Soviet* army or another, earlier one of ours—Red, White, czarist—and on which side Arnold stood and who was trying to put him to death there. It seemed to me that Arnold had been rescued throughout every possible war; only later was I able to situate his rescues in the right time and the right war, and it took me even longer to understand that Arnold was a Jew—or was regarded as Jewish—and that everything that happened to him and to them had to do with that central fact. I found out only recently that his name had once been Abram. Today I think that my whole life would have been different, wittier, and more Jewish if I had known from the start that we'd had an Abrasha in the family, a name that I associated not with real life but only with jokes that culminated in such endless episodes as Arnold's tales of survival, and maybe these tales survived only because of the jokes.

As the war drew near, Abram wanted to flee Kiev, but he worked so hard to arrange for the evacuation of the deaf-mute society that in the end he had neither time nor a vehicle to bring his own family and himself to safety.

When the All Jews order was posted, he went underground in the vicinity of Kiev and survived the war in rural hideouts with the help of Ukrainian peasants. Sometimes he posed as a craftsman and looked for work in villages where no one knew that he was Jewish. His Russian wife, Zinaida, and their three-year-old son, Tolya, remained behind in occupied Kiev. Perhaps he was unaware that the lucky rescues applied only to him, so he came home at night from time to time and brought food from the villages. The neighbors reported Zinaida to the police, claiming that she was in contact with partisans, or that she was hiding her Jewish husband. It was probably the neighbor boys, who were jealous that Zinaida had married the Jewish Abrasha, and when Abrasha left, had tried in vain to win her over. Zinaida was arrested and shot to death that very night; some said the Gestapo tortured her. When the police came for Zinaida, little Tolya was playing in the yard behind the house. He had the good luck to be playing on the wrong side of the house; maybe he had inherited survival from his father. The neighbor, Marusya, took the boy in and raised him during the war until Abram came back.

After the war ended, Arnold worked with deaf-mutes for the rest of his life, as a sports teacher, a custodian, and the society's administrator. Everyone loved him. He had a warmth about him that is normally found only in fairy tales, and he was enterprising, at least when it came to other people's business. What a wheeler-dealer he was when it came to his own interests became clear when he traded the name Abram for the name Arnold, in response to increasing state anti-Semitism during the postwar years, although the name Arnold sounded nearly as Jewish—a bit fancier and less conspicuous or even a bit Viennese, but no one was named Arnold apart from Jews. There's a joke about Abrasha who buys an egg for ten rubles, boils it, and resells it for ten rubles. When asked about the profit, he replies: I kept the egg stock, didn't I?

At the end of his life, Arnold married for the third time, and again gave proof of his good fortune, since even strict Ida, a severe woman fixated on saving money and keeping order, could not spoil his lucky streak. Her full first name was like that of his first wife, Zinaida; she cooked incomparably well, and every year for my birthday she sent me a box of eclairs shaped like swans so that on this day all would be in order with us too. My cousin Marina always said that she herself was fine, but her relatives! They were like figures from a picture book with their greed, shrillness, and aggression.

When Arnold died, all deaf-mute Kiev came to his funeral. Hundreds, thousands, of deaf-mute men and women, appearing calm and peaceful. It was as silent as it gets between people who understand each other with a mere look. Their deafness seemed to be nothing but a pretext for a covert burial pantomime, as though they were on the verge of breaking into dance. Arnold was their hero, their king, and their clown, and as long as he was there, nothing could go wrong.

Maybe Esther

May the Lord God let you know as many things as I don't know, Babushka always used to say. She repeated this adage with offended pride. Her grandson Marik, my father, Miron, was unusually well read. By the time he turned nine, he had already devoured hundreds of books and would ask adults questions that he thought quite simple and basic. Babushka generally had no answer, nor had she heard of the saying of Socrates, "I know that I know nothing." Maybe her saying served as a consolation to herself or as a rebuke to her clever grandson; Babushka stuck with these words, which sounded like an ancient aphorism, May the Lord God let you know as many things as I don't know. Apart from this adage, only two things remain from my great-grandmother, my father's babushka: a photograph and a story.

In August 1941, when the family fled from Kiev to escape the German army and my grandfather Semion had to go off to war, Babushka stayed home, alone on Engels Street, which led steeply down to Khreshchatyk, the magnificent main boulevard of Kiev.

Babushka was not taken along. She could barely move, and during this entire summer of the war, she had not been able to get downstairs and onto the street. Bringing her was out of the question; she would not have withstood the journey.

The evacuation seemed like a trip to the dacha, and Babushka was left behind with the understanding that they would all see each other again when the summer was over. July was time for a change, and all these people on the street were carrying suitcases and assorted bundles, as they always did in the summer; it was just the haste and the overly large number of them that gave away the fact that in spite of the season and the standard belongings people were carrying, these goings-on had absolutely nothing to do with a trip to the dacha.

I think her name was Esther, my father said. Yes, maybe Esther. I had two grandmothers, and one of them was named Esther—exactly.

What do you mean, "maybe"? I asked indignantly. You don't know what your grandmother's name was?

I never called her by name, my father replied. I said Babushka, and my parents said Mother.

Maybe Esther remained in Kiev. She had trouble getting around in the apartment, which was suddenly empty, and the neighbors brought her food. We thought, my father added, that we'd be back soon, but it took us seven years to return.

At first nothing of any consequence changed in the city. The Germans had come, that was all. When the summons—"All Jews in the city of Kiev are to report to the corner of . . ."—reached even Babushka, she started getting ready without hesitation. The neighbors tried to talk her out of it. *Don't go! You can't even walk!*

The monitoring was exhaustive. Building superintendents combed through addresses and resident lists. Schools, hospitals, orphanages, and retirement homes were searched to make sure that All Jews went, all of them, each Jew in the German and every Jew in the Russian. Arrivals were supervised by German and Ukrainian patrol units. Yet at 11 Engels Street, the superintendent was ready not to report the old woman, to overlook her, but it was not to save her from death, no, no one was thinking of death, or better yet, no one was thinking as far as death, no one was thinking what was going on through to the end, they were lagging behind the events.

Think about it: Why should an old lady set out on this path if she can't walk, even if it leads to the Promised Land? Don't go, the neighbors said. Maybe Esther insisted.

The center of the city had been on fire for days. The unceasing explosions terrified residents. Buildings burst apart with deadly regularity. First the overcrowded offices of the occupation authorities, then a movie theater in the middle of a showing, a soldiers' club, and an ammunition depot. It was never-ending. The retreating Red Army had laid mines in the buildings, and radio-controlled fuses set off explosions. A few days later, the Khreshchatyk lay in ruins. Fires blazed throughout the downtown area. The Germans, who had settled in the city almost peacefully at first, went from bewildered to flustered to frantic in the face of this unfamiliar form of partisan warfare. It seemed that the summons to All Jews was a logical consequence, retaliation against the allegedly guilty parties, as though they had not been guilty and convicted from the outset, as though this summons had been issued spontaneously, as though the sequence now unfolding had not been set long in advance. But Maybe Esther evidently knew nothing about that, or about what was going on in the city, even less than half a mile from her home.

For the bakery across the street, at the corner of Engels Street and Meringovskaya, was always open, as the neighbors told her. Only three steps down. Didn't you hear the explosions? Smell the stench of burning? See the fire?

If All, then All, she said to herself, as though it was a matter of honor. And she came down. Everything else stood still. There are no details about how she got down the stairs. Come to think of it, though, the neighbors must have helped her; how else could she have done it?

Downstairs, at the intersection, the streets were curving, growing rounder in the distance, and it could be felt that the earth does turn. Once she was on the street, she was alone.

Besides the patrol unit, no one could be seen at this moment. Maybe All were already gone. Two strapping, flaxen-haired, almost elegant men were strolling, unhurried and dutiful, at the intersection. It was bright and desolate, as in a dream. Maybe Esther walked toward them, and she saw that it was a German patrol unit.

How many Ukrainian policemen were out on the streets of Kiev to supervise the arrival of All on the first day of the operation? Nobody kept count. There were many Ukrainians, but presumably, or even certainly, Babushka would have rather approached Germans than Ukrainians, whom she distrusted. Did she have a choice?

She walked to them, but how long did this *walked* take? Here each and every one must follow his own breath.

Her *walked* developed like an epic event, not only because Maybe Esther moved like the tortoise in the aporias of Zeno, step by step, slowly but surely, so slowly that no one could catch up with her, and the slower she went, the more impossible it was to catch up to her, to stop her, to bring her back, and, above all, to overtake her. Not even the fleet-footed Achilles could have done that.

She took a few steps down Engels Street, a street formerly—and currently—named Luteranskaya after Martin Luther, a street where the loveliest trees grew, where German business-people had settled since the nineteenth century, and where two German churches had been built, one way up the street and the other at the corner of Bankovaya; one of them was right opposite my first school. Forty years after Babushka, I walked past these German churches every day.

First it was called Luteranskaya, then Engels Street—the street of Engels, or the street of angels. All those who didn't know which realm this street lay in might think it was really given over to angels. It was so impossibly steep, so precipitous, that it gave wing to anyone who headed down it. I was a Soviet child; I knew Friedrich Engels, and kept my feet grounded.

It may be that Maybe Esther's halting gait echoed an error of language. Yiddish was still the mother tongue of the older Jews in Kiev, whether they were religious and clung to tradition or followed their children straight into the bright Soviet future. Many elderly Jews were proud of their command of German, and when the Germans came, they may have thought, in spite of everything that was already being told, that hovered in the air and could no longer be dismissed as lies, that they, they in particular, were the closest relatives of the occupying troops, having that special entitlement of those for whom the word is everything. The rumors and reports coming to Kiev from Poland and Ukraine, already occupied in large part, were simply not believed. How could you possibly believe such a rumor?

Older residents still recalled the year 1918, when military turmoil and never-ending games of musical chairs to determine who would wield power were followed by the Germans marching into the city and enforcing some degree of order. And now it seemed that the Germans were restoring order. Those exact instructions in Russian: "All Jews in the city of Kiev and the surrounding area are to report to the corner of Melnik and Dekhtyarev Street (at the cemeteries) at 8:00 a.m. on Monday, September 29, 1941. Documents, money, and valuables as well as warm clothing, linens, etc. are to be brought along." Precise, clear, and comprehensible: *All*, 8:00 a.m., and the exact address. And neither the cemeteries nor the pejorative word *żyd* on the Russian posters alarmed them. Maybe it had to do with the slight nuances of the Polish and the Western Ukrainian language, which had no other word for Jews than *żyd*, which sounds so insulting in Russian. There was also something about execution there. Noncompliance—execution. In the case of theft of objects by Jews—execution. So it happened only if one didn't follow the rules.

In the time it took Babushka to walk, battles could have broken out, and Homer could have begun cataloging the ships.

One of the first stories my mother read to me and for some reason retold again and again, as though these repetitions held an instructive force, was the story of Achilles and his heel. When his mother bathed him in the river of immortality while holding him by the heel, my mother said in a coaxing voice, as though the story were already at the end, she held him by the heel, my mother said, I don't recall whether it was the left or the right one—but maybe my mother didn't even mention that, and I'm the one worrying about whether it was the left or the right one, although it doesn't matter in the slightest.

The river was cold, the infant didn't cry, it was the realm of shades, and they all looked like shades, even the chubby infant resembled a paper cutout. She bathed him in the river, my mother told me, to make him immortal, but she forgot his heel. I remember being so seized with fear at this point in the story, every time I heard it, that my soul slid into my heels, as we say in Russian when fear takes over; maybe it's safer for the soul to withdraw into the heels and stay there until the danger has passed. At this moment I could no longer move and could barely breathe. I knew that the heel that Achilles' mother was holding embodied something irreversible, something ill-fated. I also thought of the evil sorcerer from the fairy tale, Кощей Бессмертный, Koshchey Bessmertny, Koshchey the Deathless, who actually was mortal, but his death was hidden inside the point of a needle, the needle inside an egg, the egg inside a duck, the duck lived on an oak tree and the oak tree grew on an island and nobody knew where it was. But this was a bare heel!

I saw my mother's shadow on the wall, which looked like a figure on a terra-cotta amphora, and I thought of Achilles' mother, of the black River Styx, and of the dusky realm of shades, then of the wide river I crossed every day on the way to school, of our realm of shades, and again of my mother, who told the story of the fleet-footed Achilles, making it unimaginably long, epic, and meandering; she told me about Troy, about Achilles' friendship with Patroclus, and about wrath. She exclaimed the word *wrath* several times, and wrathfully went on to recount the way Achilles died because of his friendship with Patroclus, hit directly in the heel by an arrow shot by Paris and guided by Apollo. I didn't understand why Apollo, patron and protector of the muses, would guide this arrow to the place where my frightened soul was tarrying at this very moment.

And thus the story of Achilles became my own vulnerability, my weak spot, because my mother bathed me in this story, in the river of immortality, as if I could in this way have taken the shield of immortality, but she forgot my heel, the heel, where my soul, plagued by fear and sensing imminent doom, coiled up, and I knew that everyone has to have a nakedness, a heel, a soul, death—the only proof of immortality there is, in fact.

The means of transportation was actually crucial. Anyone who could, fled from Kiev. When Semion shouted for the family to be downstairs in ten minutes, the tub with the ficus plant was already on the loading platform, where the truck stood waiting. The neighbor, bewildered by the commotion, had put it there, ready to be evacuated. On the loading platform there already were two families, bags, suitcases, bundles, and now this ficus in the tub, the symbol of home and hearth. There was no place left for another family. Semion tugged at the ficus to pull it down, and pushed aside the suitcases to make space for his wife and his two sons. The ficus remained at the curb of the steep Luteranskaya.

I see the leaves of this ficus, bobbing to the beat of the world events in 1941. I owe my life to this ficus.

I am reading what my father wrote about his evacuation. It's all correct, except that the ficus he used to tell me about is missing. Everything is in the right place, just as it should be: a distraught, myopic boy—my future papa—his resolute father in a new uniform, the truck, the neighbors, the suitcases, the bundles, the commotion, the haste. Everything is there. Only the ficus in the tub is missing. When I notice the loss, the ground falls out from under my feet. The focal point of my story is gone.

And yet I see the ficus clearly in front of me, alone and abandoned outside my father's childhood home. Its leaves are trembling to the beat of the Wehrmacht marching into the city. When I hear this trampling, to which you could whistle Shostakovich, I understand that my father survived only because the ficus was removed from the truck. Of course the ficus had to be taken off. It would have been absurd if the ficus had been evacuated instead of the boy, but in the logic of the events of the time, this could have passed for normal. The very idea that this little boy would have had to stay behind in Kiev because of chance, a random, possibly even fictitious, chain of circumstances—just imagine that!—cuts the ground out from under my story, puts my very existence into question. You lose a single card, and you're out of the game.

Others of the boy's tribe, those who had remained in the city—although others of the tribe is so neutral, let's say Jews, it's easier, easier in the sense that it is better understood, as though it could be understood better, but it is, unfortunately or devastatingly, truly easier to understand, after the fact of course, only after the fact, once you know what happened afterward, but that doesn't actually justify what happened anyway, so, those who had remained in the city were rounded up in Babi Yar, or, as my mother always writes, BY, as though everyone knows what BY means, or as though she really, and I mean really, couldn't call this place by its full name. And they were shot to death there. But you surely know that. Kiev is just as far from here as Paris.

And now I know what I need my ficus for.

Papa, you forgot the ficus.

What ficus? I don't remember any ficus. Suitcases, bundles, bags, crates. But a ficus?

Papa, you did tell me about the ficus that was taken back down from the truck.

Which ficus? I don't recall that. Maybe I forgot.

I was fixated on that ficus, I was ficusated. I didn't understand how something like that could be forgotten. I didn't understand what must have happened to forget something like that.

The ficus strikes me as the main character in the history, if not of the world, then of my family. In my version, the ficus saved my father's life. But if even my father can no longer remember the ficus, maybe it didn't really exist. When he told me about the evacuation, maybe I inserted the missing details into the blanks of the street.

Did the ficus exist, or was it a fiction? Was the fiction born from the ficus, or the other way around? I may never find out whether the ficus that saved my father ever existed at all.

I call up my father, and he comforts me.

—Even if it didn't exist, these kinds of mistakes sometimes tell us more than a painstaking inventory. Sometimes that pinch of poetry is the very thing that makes memory truth.

And so my fictive ficus was vindicated as a literary subject.

Less than a week had gone by when my father said to me, I think I recall a ficus. Maybe I do. Or did I get the ficus from you?

If my grandfather hadn't taken down this dubious ficus from the loading platform, the nine-year-old boy who later became my father wouldn't have had room in the ark of the truck, he wouldn't have wound up on the list of the survivors, and I wouldn't exist. Since there was no ficus, but we are here, it means that it was there after all, or in any case it must have been there, because if it had not been, there would be no "us," we wouldn't have been able to rescue ourselves, I'm saying "we" to mean my father, because if my father hadn't been rescued, how could he have recalled the ficus, and how could he have forgotten this ficus earlier? So it turned out—or it could turn out—that we owe our life to a fiction.

Kherr Offizehr, Babushka began with her distinctive guttural enunciation, convinced that she was speaking German, *zeyn Zi so fayn,* kindly tell me, *was zoll ikh denn machen,* what should I do? *Ikh hob di plakatn gezen mit instruktzies far jidn,* I saw the posters with instructions for Jews, but I cannot walk too well, *ikh kann nyscht loyfn azoy schnel.*

She was shot on the spot, as a careless matter of routine, without the officers interrupting their conversation, without turning around all the way, nonchalantly. Or no, no. Maybe she said, Please be so kind, *Kherr Offizehr,* and tell me how to get to Babi Yar? Now that would have been annoying. Who likes having to answer stupid questions?

I observed this scene like God out of the window of the building across the street. Maybe that's how people write novels. Or fairy tales. I sit up there and see everything! Sometimes I screw up my courage, draw near, and stand behind the officer's back to listen in on the conversation. Why are they standing with their backs to me? I go around them and see nothing but their backs. No matter how hard I try to see their faces, to peer into the faces of Babushka and the officer, no matter how far I stretch out to take a look at them, straining all the muscles of memory, imagination, and intuition—it does not work. I don't see their faces, don't understand, and the history books maintain their silence.

How do I know every detail of this story? Where did I listen to it? Who whispers unwitnessed stories to us, and for what reason? Does it matter that this old woman is my father's babushka? And what if this wasn't the grandmother he loved?

There actually *were* witnesses to this story. In 1948 my father's family returned to Kiev, seven years after the dacha-like evacuation, after stays in Rostov and Ashgabat, and spending several years in Barnaul in the Altai region. The house on Engels Street was destroyed, as was the entire neighborhood. All that remained of the building was a shell, a skeleton. On the fifth-floor balcony there was a bed, but there was no way to get to it. The interior of the house was gone, and so was the staircase. A German aerial photograph taken in November 1941 shows this bed where my nine-year-old father had sunbathed during the first summer of the war.

When Maybe Esther made her way alone, walking against time, there were many invisible witnesses to our story: passersby, the salesladies in the bakery three steps down, and the neighbors behind the curtains of this densely populated street, unmentioned, faceless masses for refugee processions. They are the last storytellers. Where did they all move to?

My grandfather Semion spent a long time looking for people who knew something about Babushka. The superintendent of the building that was no longer there told him everything. I think that on this twenty-ninth of September 1941, there was someone standing at the window. Maybe.

CHAPTER 6

DEDUSHKA

Grandfather's Silence

He smiled meekly, bashful about his happiness, as though his sitting there was the apex of his existence. He sat in his armchair, smiled at his grandchildren, and kept his silence. It was conceivable that it was not only his character but his life that had granted him his peace of mind. In June 1941 he went off to war, wound up in an encirclement near Kiev, spent almost four years as a prisoner of war, and survived, but did not return to his family. Forty-one years later, I witnessed his homecoming from the war.

The madwoman in the tram was right. Outside it was already the 1980s, but as the tram rounded a curve, she asked first the people sitting next to her, then the fat, sweaty ticket taker, then me, the eleven-year-old, how the war had turned out and whether it had ever ended. She asked about the end of the war in the way one might ask about a streetcar stop, as though where she got off depended on the answer. Is the war over?

Half a year later, my grandfather came back. For a long time I had not had a grandfather, and all of sudden, there he was. First I visited him in his garden, then he moved to our house; Home, he said, I want to go home.

Of all the people to wind up in a camp, in Mauthausen, I was told, it was my grandfather, the only Ukrainian in the family.

Once he was back in the Soviet Union, he was sent to a filtration camp and interrogated there. A woman helped him escape from our camps. *Our camps* sounded almost tender to me; I didn't know that there was a thud of a word for it: gulag. No one used that word at the time. My grandfather stayed with the woman who had rescued him, a clear and logical matter, they told me; after all, she did save him. He stayed with her, lived in Kiev, and did not return to his family, to his Rosa and their two daughters, who were then ten and eighteen years old. I was twelve when he came back, after an absence of four decades. He spent all his time sitting in his armchair and smiling. One year later he died at home.

Everything in this compact version was true. A few lines of his life ran by me in the rhythm of a ballad. I didn't ask any questions, and I didn't entertain any doubts. He was gone, and now he was here.

I repeated his story to myself, then and later, as though learning it by heart, yet something remained unclear and bothered me. Was it his stellar career in the ministry of agriculture? The camp? The return? Before the war, he had risen through the ranks as an agriculturist and veterinary scientist; he was a reliable worker, good-looking and attractive, and he was popular with the ladies. Sometime in the mid-1930s, he was appointed to a high post in the ministry of agriculture, traveled to the Baltic for conferences, bought breeding cattle there for Ukraine, clothing and silk stockings for Rosa, his second wife. He was not indicted for his trips abroad during the Great Purge. Maybe he didn't go to the Baltic while it was still foreign, going only once it was a part of our one big coerced family, after the Pact, when the war had already broken out for the Balts and not yet for us.

When I got to know my grandfather, he was tall and lean, and had finely chiseled features and pale blue eyes, looking more like an elegant German elder, the way I pictured old German men, than a Soviet pensioner and former agriculturalist. He rarely spoke, and then only to say *da* or *khorosho*, and he seemed to speak with an accent; the words that came out of his mouth sounded so odd and alien. It was a strange feeling to get a grandfather at the age of twelve, almost as though he had been born after me.

His smile nurtured his silence. No stories about the war, not a word about the past, about experiences, no *Those were the days*. Today it strikes me as peculiar that we didn't question him about what had happened to him, we children of the 1970s, who were saturated with the spirit of this war, the most important introduction to world history, a war that imposed a "sentimental education," loss and love, friendship and betrayal, we drew from the well of this war, which never ran dry.

On May 9, Victory Day, four of my girlfriends and I were standing in front of the subway station to welcome the war veterans. Thousands of them were coming past us as they made their way from the parade in the center of the city to their homes, their bedroom communities. We had saved up the money that our parents had given us for cake and ice cream, we had saved every kopek for months, and bought hundreds of postcards and flowers. On May 9, daffodils cost only three kopeks apiece, and tulips five kopeks.

We wrote the postcards after school, for hours at a time, extending over three weeks. *Dear Veteran! We send you best wishes on the occasion of this joyous celebration!* When we saw the old men—and often women as well—with their medals, we ran up to them and handed them a postcard and a flower, not at the ritualistic ceremonies in front of the monuments, not at school, when the veterans came to visit us and tell their stories, no, at a subway station next to Hotel Tourist. The most astonishing part was the voluntary nature of our action. We had done exactly what our ideologues at school had demanded of us, namely honor the war veterans, but we had skirted any coercion, we had done it in spite of having been granted permission to do so, and we sensed that we were doing something revolutionary. No one had ordered us, no one had given us the idea, no one had praised us. We felt like mavericks. We extended our greetings wholeheartedly to those who had saved us according to the official Soviet dictum, which was actually true in this war of extermination. Who could claim that we were adhering to Soviet war propaganda? The veterans asked us who had sent us, because they, too, sensed that we were breaking the rules.

And yet I missed my grandfather. He was nowhere to be found in this throng of heroic honorees; he had no medals and didn't join the crowds that, on Victory Day, sang and danced and recalled their wild wartime youth. And I didn't question the matter. People didn't even mention the millions of prisoners of war in this context; the term was reserved for the Germans who had to rebuild Kiev after the war. Our prisoners of war were excluded from the Great Patriotic War and erased from memory. No wonder my grandfather didn't exist. He was from a different story, a different war.

It was forbidden to be captured, and if you were captured, it was forbidden to survive. That was an unspoken Soviet aporia of war. Survival is the mark of a traitor; death is better than treachery. Hence, any returning prisoner of war is a traitor and stands to be punished. These syllogisms were drummed into us with the inevitability of ancient logic; there was no getting around them, so classical did they appear, these sentences carved out for eternity; if you are not with us, you are against us, although the state forgot to explain that it was itself to blame that the soldiers had lacked ammunition, that they fought with outdated technology, and that it was our great strategists who allowed the encirclement of their army of millions.

Between the armies near Kiev and the armchair in our apartment, a black hole opens up.

Lunch Break in Mauthausen

The clock says nine minutes to twelve when I dial the phone to Mauthausen, a former concentration camp and now a memorial site. For a long time, nobody picks up. The phone rings and rings out there. I get the feeling that I'm calling up the past, and no one is around.

It's not every day that I call up a concentration camp. To be honest, it's my first time. The working hours are listed on the Internet. Lunch break from twelve to one. So they ought to be working for another nine minutes. Have I become that German? I let it ring and ring on the other end. I've opened up another website on my screen so I can shop for Christmas presents.

I picture the room at the other end. With every ring the space expands outward, a standard office becoming an endless tunnel. My eyes make out the winding staircase, the shadows, the backlighting. Hitchcock or Orson Welles, a touch of vertigo, a funnel. That's how I am imagining the office of the Mauthausen memorial site.

As the funnel is about to swallow me up, the ringing stops, and I hear a woman's voice in the distance. In her brisk Austrian accent, she tells me something and hangs up. I need a moment to grasp the fact that this was not an answering machine.

I am the customer. The woman on the other end is the customer service. She works, and I receive the fruits of her labor. I know that at the end of what the woman said, there was something about "no one is answering." She didn't give me the chance to ask her how it was that no one is answering if she was speaking to me at that very moment.

I dial the number again. After a long wait, the same woman is there again. She spits out the same perfectly polished line a second time. After her "No one is answering" I quickly say, Why not? On the computer screen, I see six contact people listed for Mauthausen, located not in Mauthausen but in Vienna, at the ministry of the interior. We're on lunch break, she says. There are nine minutes left, I say. I'm lying; it's already seven minutes to twelve. They don't eat exactly according to the clock, she says. Should I call back in an hour? You can try that. I don't think of asking the woman why she can't speak to me herself if she's already speaking to me. What does *Arbeit* do to people, anyway?

The Garden

Some in their wanderings
Come to this portal on dusky paths.
Golden blooms the tree of grace
From the earth's cool sap.

—GEORG TRAKL

My grandfather Vasily Ovdiyenko, whom I called Dedushka Vasya, was known as Ded Vasya to everyone else; they felt that nicknames weren't appropriate for him. In 1982, when he turned up in the family again after his war odyssey, he had brought along his garden. It was a miracle, a stroke of luck, a bit of normality. It seemed as though everyone else had a garden, a little dacha, a bit of land—a quarter of an acre—and a babushka in the country, but not us. Anyone with some money or a job in a factory or a scholarly institute with a nice-sounding name had a dacha, as did rank-and-file officers, engineers, saleswomen, doctors, construction workers—especially the workers. We were the only ones who didn't. It was our lack of money, our inability to purchase a dacha, but I thought it was the curse of the books. We had thousands of books, which came with us every time we moved, and the only reason we were still at all able to breathe in our apartment was that family friends occasionally did not return books they had borrowed from us. We were cursed by books, I figured, and I dreamed of a babushka with a colorful scarf on her head and callused black hands, of a garden with apple trees, of a bit of land to grow flowers on that belonged to me alone. Maybe I was reacting to the torpor in my agrarian society, where belonging came with owning a bit of land. I would have been satisfied with a rose on a little planet; I would have taken care of it, I would have gone without sleep for it, and I would have breathed only for it, like the Little Prince. But we had no one who lived in the countryside for us, we didn't have a bit of land, and we shared a single planet with all of mankind. My mother taught, my father wrote, and the flowers on the balcony were no consolation.

Then suddenly there was a grandfather, a farmer, a Ukrainian. He had a garden, so I had a garden too. Everyone else had only dachas, the same dacha paradise everywhere, a quarter of an acre, with a cabin, a vegetable patch, and practical things, from herbs to tomatoes, to sweeten their survival. My grandfather had a garden full of roses.

To get to the garden we took the tram, the new rapid-transit one, which brought us to my grandfather's on a long but straight route. This part of town, far from the center, was the only place with that futuristic fairground attraction: the tracks had neither joints nor railings, and the tram kept going without applying the brakes at intersections or turning off at small streets. It was as impetuous as a bird in the sky, an impetuous flight all the way to the last station, and through the window I saw the high-rises, the factories, the famous institute for aircraft construction—the ugliest advances of our ugly civilization. Even this was a place where people lived. Before the tram turned around and flew off just as insouciantly in the other direction, entrapped by tracks that never changed course, it made a brief stop, and we got out. Who's we? I don't recall anyone getting out with me. There was only me, and my grandfather was waiting for me in his garden.

And so I walked toward him, through the big dacha development with all these people who were giving a second life to their old clothing: tattered trousers, summer skirts with parted zippers, worn-out shoes, the women often wore their linen underclothes, doesn't matter if we're seen, we're on our own private property. Many of them spent eternities at their fences, shelling sunflower seeds and, like the sunflowers, facing toward the sun, and when the sun went down, they were like nightshades, like the evil tomatoes in the children's book. They were an unperturbed, unapologetic, humdrum community. I was a little afraid of them; I didn't know their laws. I wanted to be one of them so I could turn in the direction of the sun as well. They stared at us unblinkingly; we looked far too urban, anti-dacha, and different. They knew something about life that we didn't. We could never adapt, we could not put down roots, we could not even slow down, we forged ahead like birds. At the end of the development, at the edge of the field near the woods, was my grandfather's garden.

Dozens of kinds of roses blossomed there, yellow, white, red, pink, almost black ones, small vermilion ones, purple, brown. Not once have I seen roses like this even in the most beautiful flowerbeds in honor of the Soviet achievements. Our botanical gardens were full of roses from around the world with little labels that bore the oddest names: they told of foreign lands, lost worlds, and our unformed longing, and these, too, were blossoming. In the large garden of our country, as much as possible was grafted for decades, especially varieties of apples, at the same time as steps were being taken to decrease human varieties.

Grandfather had the variety of paradise apple tree called Fame for the Victors, a true juicy pleasure of the victory over fascism. But he was no victor. The closest he came was his apple tree in the middle of his garden, looking like a gallant dwarf among giants.

I already had my Garden of Eden in the center of the city. At the end of the street I was born on and where my grandmother had lived before the war, there was a palace, the former Institute for Daughters of the Nobility, which was later renamed the October Palace. In its left wing I danced for years, in its right wing I sang for years. In front of the palace there were hundreds of tea roses in all possible colors. We knew that what belongs to everyone belongs to no one, and so I took them under my wing. I also adopted the hill on which the palace stood, from the great Nobody, for my own purposes. I spent years of my childhood sitting on this beautiful hill in Kiev, above the most important street of the city, directly overlooking the Maidan. Tuesdays, Thursdays, Saturdays: ballet; Wednesdays, Fridays, Sundays: choir. On the hill, between ancient chestnuts and fragrant shrubbery, in a small glade, was a paradise apple tree. Tiny bitter fresh apples, which we ate up in a single bite, including the core.

In the spring the entire hillside was full of wild violets. In the middle of the city, nature reigned victorious, it reigned victorious and I spent my best hours of boredom on this hill, and later, much later, I thought of it again when I heard the Russian rock band Aquarium's song "Sitting on a Beautiful Hill."

At the time I first heard this song, I learned that in the 1930s, my palace had been the central torture chamber of the NKVD, the People's Commissariat for Internal Affairs, where thousands had been shot to death. My beautiful hill drifted away from me, drenched in crimson, fertilized with bitter paradise apples, which now seemed to me nothing but blood. The shootings took place on the other side of the hill, a historian recently explained to me, as though that would render my apples untainted and I would be spared the fall from grace. Whenever I think of paradise apples, there's an aftertaste in my mouth, as if even the apples in my grandfather's garden had been contaminated with alien blood. He had already been working in agriculture in the 1930s, when the Great Famine broke out as a result of collectivization, which was to wipe out the peasantry as a whole. And he, so eager and adept that he advanced to the position of deputy director of the Kiev region for cattle breeding at the very time that Ukraine, "the land of the black earth," began to die, he, who so dearly loved the animals and the earth—was even he complicit?

On the edge of my grandfather's garden, there grew huge white raspberries, a sort I have never seen anywhere else. There were red roses and white roses, and no war between them. Chinese tea roses and October Stars, Great Loves, and many with names unfamiliar to me, such as Gloria Dei (I figured Dei was the last name of a lovely lady), Gamburg (where is Gamburg?), and, of course, Dolce Vita. My grandfather stood at the center of this rose garden, next to his little cabin. And when I now recall that and try to enter this fragrant and buzzing garden kingdom, I'm unable to do so; I see only the framed picture, the roses, the bushes, the raspberries, and the paradise apple tree. I try to stick my head into this picture like Alice in Wonderland: *I'll get into the garden!* All I want is this garden, blended together with all the fairy tales of the world, with its secret paths and tracks of unknown animals. *The Name of the Rose, Gloria Dei, a rose is a rose, Dolce Vita.*

In the middle of this paradise, at the edge of the field, is my silent, smiling, contented grandfather, cultivating his garden.

Friday Letters

> I heard a voice coming from the shore: "Come, come, Russky," and I saw a German soldier pointing his weapon at me. I begged him: "Please don't kill me, my mother has no one but me"; I spoke Russian, he didn't understand me, he just had sympathy, in any case he didn't shoot, and helped me out of the water and onto the shore, and then he waited until I had recovered a little and brought me to the other prisoners. This is how life began in the Nazi camps.

Every Friday I receive an e-mail from a Soviet prisoner of war, in German translation, an e-mail from one of the many listservs that flood my mailbox. Over the past few years the letters were written, collected, translated mostly by volunteers, and then sent out via the listservs, numbered consecutively like the prisoners. There were more than five million Soviet prisoners of war, two-thirds of whom died.

> Every morning we woke up and found dead people lying on both sides of us. Anyone who was still alive got up and went to work, and the dead were all thrown into a pit.

> Then a kindhearted farmer took me with him. For the first few days he gave me easy work and I was well fed. I quickly regained my strength. The farmer's name was Heinrich S.

> During the entire six days' journey they got a single bucket of water for the entire car only once. . . . When they arrived, half of the prisoners had already died. . . . They set the dogs on the prisoners . . . One guard came to the rescue of a prisoner . . . at the edge of an open ditch. . . . The doctors who were there said, "Oh, just go ahead and die." I hated the totalitarian regime of the pockmarked Georgian, but the idea of fighting against my own people wasn't enticing. . . . 50 grams of bread with wood shavings . . . at some point we reached Wriezen . . . "Toni, Germany is a musical country. Won't you tell me who Leo Blech is?"

The messages are sent out between five and eight in the morning, one every Friday. Since getting an iPhone, I've been reading them in bed, in the morning. Facebook messages from night owls blend into a morning greeting from a prisoner of war. Who reads these letters with me, every Friday at 7:00 a.m. in bed; who shares my Friday ritual with me?

Dozens, hundreds of places are named: Königsberg, Nuremberg, Küstrin, Bielefeld, Hanover, Munich, Bochum, Graz, Strasbourg. Every Friday I hope to get a letter that names the stations of my grandfather: September 1941, encirclement near Kiev, one and a half years transit camp, Volodymyr-Volynsky, as of the summer of 1943 internment camp Stalag XVIII C in St. Johann im Pongau, as of March 8, 1945, Mauthausen, as of March 25, 1945, Gunskirchen. St. Johann is mentioned in two letters, one letter refers to Volodymyr-Volynsky in Western Ukraine. Almost all of them died there during the first winter, but not my grandfather.

Pearls

From the right path I found myself astray.

—DANTE

My grandfather Vasily Ovdiyenko's Mauthausen registration card, numbered 137616, states "Russ. civilian," not "Soviet officer"; his wife was listed as Natalia Hutorna and not Rosalia Krzewina, and instead of "Communist" it said "Russ. Orthodox." Only the address was right: Institutskaya 44. My grandfather wanted to survive, and was persistent about it. I looked for the former stalag for prisoners of war outside Salzburg, and for the Russian cemetery, and I waged an unequal battle with the Internet and its vacation packages. I found the places I was looking for, but they were the settings of hiking trails, swimming pools, and vacation homes for the whole family. There is an itinerary for lovers and itineraries for families, and where there are vacation homes, there must be families to fill them, especially in Austria. St. Johann im Pongau, fifty minutes by train from Salzburg. A vacation home, another vacation home, swimming pools, fun, fun, fun.

I traveled alone, intending to ignore the land opening out in front of me. I was not to see more than my grandfather was able to see back then.

The Salzburg Stapo, or security police, transferred him from the stalag to Mauthausen in March 1945. Then, he, a Ukrainian by the name of Ovdiyenko, went to Gunskirchen, together with Bourdier, Kurtág, Zibulski, Brioni, Holländer, Borchuladze: a Frenchman, a Hungarian, a Pole, an Italian, a German, a Georgian—an exemplary Internationale, which left the overcrowded Mauthausen camp on March 25, 1945, and marched to Gunskirchen, fifty-five kilometers on foot. A disconcerting Internationale; it was as though the dreams of fraternity and unity had reached their pinnacle in the concentration camp, as though it was the concentration camp that had made them come true. Auschwitz had already been liberated, yet the small Gunskirchen camp was still under construction. In late April, Hungarian Jews took the same route from Mauthausen to Gunskirchen as my grandfather had shortly before that, the death march of the Hungarian Jews, two weeks before the end of the war.

I walk through the country like a rambler, dream like a

vagabond, a sleepwalker with a haversack, joyful, hovering, empty for the future, yet with a faint suspicion that I am being punished for something, perhaps for this ease, my jolly gait a mere outgrowth of what happened here, many years ago. I walk on foot with measured step, the way poems are written, adhering to an inner rhythm, because all Russian poems about walking the road are written in trochaic pentameters. *Vy-kho-zhu-o-din-ya-na-do-ro-gu* / I walk out alone upon the road.

In this dream I was so naive that, as mountains and valley changed places with the rhythm of my breath, I didn't see the paved roads, but drove through an Austria of my dreams, along a dusty roadside choked with weeds, and cars passed by me, cars, even brand-new ones that had driven straight from TV ads into my dream, full of people traveling from here to there, who knew precisely where and why they were driving past me, and I was touched by the churning dust and wrapped into its plumes, they reached the destination much more quickly than I because they knew where it was, or rather because they regarded the point of their arrival as the destination, and the destination as the solution. I abandoned myself to the path like to the current of a river, through wide valleys sprawling like drowsy women, revealing ever new lines of the landscapes. I was engulfed by the green, the sun, the blue sky. The rapeseed fields were so yellow that I had to blink with happiness. In this dream of rambling, I even forgot that I am a woman, and wandered about like a journeyman with his bundle, forgetting myself completely and seeing only the path ahead.

When I woke up, I studied maps. Austria looks like a slightly aroused aging phallus. I looked for Mauthausen, then the outposts of Mauthausen, then Stalag XVIII C (317). In Russian, centuries are written in Roman numerals: when I see Stalag XVIII, I think of the eighteenth century, the Enlightenment, the Hermitage in St. Petersburg, Catherine the Great. The map on the Internet listed all the camps on Austrian soil, prisoner-of-war camps, work camps, and concentration camps. Austria is studded with little dots, like the sky on a clear night. Hundreds of little dots, myriads, with names and functions. If one were to expand the map to the scale of reality, it might be possible to grasp how the people didn't know what was happening in the neighboring village, because there are thousands of light-years that lie between the stars, but in the scale of my search these were too many dots, far too many for this lovely land.

I dreamed of green velvet carpets of alpine-meadow splendor from various empires and royal families, adorned with pearls and garnets lying atop the fresh soft green velvet. I embroidered little gemstones onto the velvet, in gold, green, dark red, white. The images were predetermined, enigmatic ornaments, constellations never seen by the human eye; the embroidering took a lot of work or wizardry. When I woke up, everything was finished, as in the fairy tales about Vasilisa the Wise, who cooked, sewed, and wove while the others were asleep, for the morning is wiser than the evening. I marveled at my work, my wizardry.

In the morning, when this dream also faded and the green velvet went back to being the map of Austria, the pearls turned back into the outposts of Mauthausen.

In the airplane I read Thomas Bernhard, convinced that I had to attain a certain level of knowledge to enter the country, or the customs officers wouldn't let me in. I have no need to work up my fear, I hear the shouting on Heldenplatz and see the cheering crowd, as though I was standing at the edge of the square. The shouting from back then is drowning out the sound of the airplane motor, and the past is weighing on me like a sultry dream. If I do not wake up now, I'll suffocate.

At Grandfather's

The people are sitting on bunk pallets. I am standing at the threshold. There aren't many people; there ought to be far more. It ought to be jam-packed. The barracks are endlessly long; I don't know if they ever come to an end, I see only the first rows of the pallets. My grandfather ought to be here, right here. You always think that the one you're looking for is dutifully sitting in the front row. All you have to do is show up, and you'll be recognized and greeted on the spot. Welcome to Mauthausen! Step right in!

I do not step in. I stop at the threshold. The people look at me. They are all eyes. They look at me as though I am the messiah. I am standing exactly where he would come in, at the threshold. They're waiting for the messiah. I want them to wait. I wish to give them some air.

I pull colorful ribbons out of my pants pockets, more and more of them. Bright colors on the faded black and white.

Like a clown. I can do anything. They wait. I'm helpless. I keep pulling colorful ribbons out of my pockets, hoping to spread a little joy. How am I supposed to behave here? Here, in the concentration camp.

I didn't want to go inside the barracks, smell that air, see those bodies. Now we are going in without knocking, as though we're taking a stroll. Just because there are no doors? I wish to protect these people from our gaze, sew them curtains. Veils.

My grandfather was a farmer, a cattle breeder. What did he think of these barracks? I try to make him out in these rows of eyes. I try to decipher faces. Here you can only count. But I'm not good at counting. I do not know exactly what would have to be added or completed to make a normal face, to recognize a human being.

Everyone has those eyes.

There really ought to be filth everywhere. I read about it. Death ought to reek. But I smell nothing. I hear nothing. I just see. They are ghosts. It's true, they are not all good people. You have to distinguish. But what for, they're all here already.

I look for my grandfather. I've come to pick him up. I know that he now weighs 108 pounds. Still, that doesn't make him stand out here. No one weighs more. Do you think that this image is unbefitting? Never fear; it befits the situation. *Befits* is a word I learned quite recently. *The artistic concept of our information site addresses the catastrophe with befitting dignity.*

Unbearable, you might say. It is unbearable. But there is no word for the unbearable. If the word bears it, it's bearable.

We remain at the threshold. Here everything is befitting, the barracks, the prisoners' weight, the eyes. Someone has to have come up with all of this, someone with a sense of proportion. A farmer? An architect? An optometrist?

What am I doing here, anyway? What brings me here? Everything was taken from these people, everyone says, and I say so too. I am standing at the threshold where the executioner's foot has trod.

My grandfather is sitting in these barracks. Does that grant me special rights? Is that an invitation? An excuse? A mission? I am not being catapulted into the past. It's happening now. When, where, and with whom it happens is not the issue.

Who am I here? May I have a look?

My husband says, You're there as the granddaughter, you may

My father says, You have a difficult task

My brother says, Research, research, research

My mother says, Your brain is mush, but your heart is good

My friend says, *War and Peace* is also written in two different languages, in the language of war and in the language of peace

My angel says it is to be continued. Then he blows his trumpet

My grandfather sits in silence and smiles
There is no message from God. Not a peep

And I stay where I am, at this threshold. I don't find my grandfather in these barracks. I had hoped he would wave to me and whisper, *Here, here, I'm here!*

Milky Way

I wanted to read about churches and museums, but my first hit was the book *In the Shadow of the Mozartkugel*, about places in Salzburg that are associated with the Nazi past. The search engine knows my preferences—catastrophes first. In the region of Salzburg alone, there were 33,000 registered Nazis, exactly as many as the murdered Jews in the first massacre in my hometown. Nature loves symmetry, and so does history.

My grandfather may have spent only a single day in Salzburg. Why was he the only one transferred to Mauthausen? Did he work with farmers and try to flee? Historians think he should then have been sent to Dachau. Why aren't they surprised that he wasn't killed right away? Everywhere people were being killed or left to die, why was it necessary to bother with a single person at all?

Just as I was pondering these questions, my telephone stopped working, as though someone had cut off my umbilical cord to the universe. I took it personally. The cosmos no longer seemed to be supporting my undertaking, and I had my doubts as to whether trains would still be going to St. Johann if even my telephone wasn't working anymore.

At the shop of Austria's largest cell phone service provider, a woman explained to me that I wasn't her customer, and when I explained that I absolutely had to make a telephone call and asked if she could help me, *Please, there aren't any pay phones in Salzburg*, she said no, and she was right, I wasn't her customer, her actual customers wouldn't get upset over the smallest injustice the way I did, and no means no, I kept asking her for help or a solution as though it was a matter of life or death to make the call, as though I was about to have a baby or a heart attack, I vividly imagined my dying and her saying No, only for customers, and anyone who gets as worked up as I do, as if it were about the ability to kill, just because I'm not getting the help I need, can't be a customer, because if I were her customer, I could have been helped, she was not to blame that I had to go, I was to blame that I was not her customer, I didn't belong in the brightly lit paradise of her store between the house of Mozart and the house of Trakl, I had no connection to geniuses, or even a network.

But the trains were running. I took one to St. Johann im Pongau and rode through the tranquil landscape. The conductor was chitchatting with a Kuwaiti businessman in English, *well met, Austria*, and the river followed our quick movement like my secret ally, at the bridges there were canisters of milk with "www.milch.com" across their bellies, milk that flowed in the Internet, in white streams, while I still had no network, no access to the breasts of the universe, no security, although I don't even drink milk, but I was following the Milky Way, the Milky Way of a farmer and cattle breeder.

Maybe nature has long rooted every sort of violence in its circulatory system, the heavy steps of the armies marching through, the rich villages dying of hunger, the shell holes, the burials, and the unburied, and in the very place we seek serenity, this transformation has already taken place; with every breath and every bite of an apple we become a part of it, a part of the pollution and the sin that we didn't commit, even ignorance of the laws of nature cannot free us from this sin. If Cain killed Abel and Abel didn't have any children, who, then, are we?

Russian Cemetery

Mortality differs
On the right and the left side of the railway.

—ERICH FRIED

This access road has existed for only a few years; a history teacher in St. Johann im Pongau fought for it and also the sign on the state road, Russian Cemetery, just under an hour past Salzburg. You head down, anticipating something Russian Orthodox, something opulent with crosses and gold, only to find nothing but obelisks with a red star on top. On the left are five graves for officers, in the middle a large memorial for a nameless three thousand, then a memorial for thirty-one dead and two monuments for Serbs, who are listed by name. The liberators set this up shortly after the war; no one knows exactly when and according to what plan.

At first French people were brought to Stalag XVIII, then Serbs. In 1941 Soviet prisoners of war began to come, two-thirds of whom died on the journey. The French were permitted to work and eat in the South Compound; they were able to worship, had their own sports field, a newspaper of their own, *Le Stalag XVIII C vous parle*, they put on plays and got to watch movies, they received mail and packages of food from the Red Cross. On Bastille Day, the Marseillaise resounded over St. Johann, which was then called Markt Pongau. The Soviet prisoners in the North Compound, by contrast, the allies of the French, ate grass. They died of malnutrition and disease, they were treated worse than cattle, beasts of burden were a product of civilization, not so Bolsheviks. My grandfather was lucky not to be Jewish; the Jewish soldiers and officers had already been executed in the Volodymyr-Volynsky camp, and now he also survived the North Compound of Stalag XVIII.

The cemetery is nestled in a glen between the state road and the Salzach River, a safe and secure spot, like the hollow of a hand. I, too, felt safe and secure here in the fresh greenery, in the shadow of the trees between the monuments. The Russian names missing from the obelisks can be found in the files. Students at the local high school spent years conducting research with their teacher to "give back the names" to the deceased without any official assignment or encouragement. They accepted this legacy by choice, because it had to do with their home.

The guest book is housed in a cottage, as is the list with the names of the buried.

For so many years, I have been commemorating the presence of all those who lie buried here when I ride by. Now, for the first time, I am standing here, and the inner grandeur and tranquillity of this place are indescribable. Thanks to those who take care of this site! If I could do something, I would construct a fountain with fresh, clear, life-giving water, as a sign that the calvaries of our world never have the last word.

Next to the guest book are the notebooks of the Austrian Black Cross, charged with setting up dignified burial sites for the war dead; its website urges "reconciliation over the graves."

I was also a prisoner of war, first at Borodino, then in Moscow, and I am remembering the Soviet soldiers and my fellow soldiers, many of whom died in captivity.

It is not by chance that I found myself here on a Good Friday

Chance led me and my dog here

мой отец был здесь

we're here thanks to the Internet

Why is it called a Russian cemetery if there are Serbs here as well?

My father was here

pocivajte v miru

I visited here as my grandpa . . .

In grosser Dankbarkeit und Trauer

à la mémoire du mon grand-père

The book has been here for three years. The children and grandchildren of the prisoners of war continue to come—or are now starting to do so. Adi, who was born during the war as Adolf, maintains the cemetery; he has created an idyll, as though hoping to reconcile with his name by tending to these graves.

Again we returned to this hallowed site and we are glad to see the entries of so many visitors. We escaped Hitler's Holocaust in 1939 but lost all our relatives in Poland. We hope for peace.

Here we think of the poor Soviet prisoners of war, and of my first husband, who is missing in Stalingrad.

The entry is dated July 24, 2010. Sixty-seven years after the Battle of Stalingrad, this woman writes "is missing," as though she just received this notice.

Hans

My grandfather was born in Rivne, which means something like "plain," a smooth flatland. He worked in Rivne, in Kiev, and in rural Western Ukraine. Although he had held a high position before the war, no papers could be found, and no one knew any specifics about his activities. Only his time as a prisoner of war was accessible to me; there was concrete evidence for it, and its course unfolded for me on my travels, the walks around the stalag. I dreamed of walks through the countryside; he had worked the land, and where else would I find him but in the countryside?

We traveled toward Flachau, another place with *plain* in its name; our group consisted of the history teacher who had campaigned for the cemetery, the historian Michael, whose parents had been tenants at the estate of Count Plaz and knew everything about the history of the area, the writer O. P. Zier, and me. I had never really gone *wandern*; my mother tongue doesn't even have an apt expression for that kind of rambling: in Russian we can only go on a pilgrimage or for a stroll. Where our hiking trail began, only twenty yards from the parking lot, several women were sitting on the ground with a large group of children, all dressed in black. We smiled uncertainly. Saudis, Michael said knowledgeably. What are they doing here on the street? They're cooling off, Michael explained; they sit down, always at the beginning of the hiking trails, and stay there. They arrive by airplane from their scorching cities, take the train and then their cars, and now they have arrived at the place that is our starting point.

Last year, said Michael, there were Orthodox Jews from Israel here. They, too, came with dozens of children, all dressed in black like the Saudis, in midsummer, in complete disregard for the weather. When it started to rain, they all ran onto the street. The locals stayed indoors, but the foreigners went outside and rejoiced at the rain, the Saudis and the Jews.

We walked along a little brook that was louder than it looked, to see Hans, a farmer who lived in the mountains, all alone, without his wife, Michael told us. Hans had explained that the air down in the valley was too heavy for him, and for her, the air up in the mountains was too thin.

As we approached the house, a giant came toward us, so tall that his shadow ran over mountain peaks. This was Hans, with the sparkling eyes of an adventurer, hirsute as a robber, masculine, all-too-masculine, the sort of man who ought to get up and go out into the world, to kill and to rescue. But he could not leave his farm. Hans was wearing heavy boots with red laces and a Soviet cap with a hammer and sickle on the red star. *Look out, a granddaughter of a Soviet prisoner of war in the area!* the mountains had called out to him. Sure enough, he really was prepared for my arrival and launched right into stories, as though we had hired him to give a tour. A Russian prisoner of war, back in World War I, carved this cross, Hans explained, and showed us a fragile wooden Russian Orthodox cross next to the door. The Russian lived here and fell in love with a girl from the valley; they had a son, Hans said, and glanced at us as though amused by the simplicity of the events and the steadfast laws of nature, and then the prisoner left, Hans said, for his hometown, his son grew up without him, and in the next war this son went over to the Nazis, and how! Hans said, and looked at us triumphantly, with a show of pride, but it was his story that he was proud of—and then he went to Dachau or Mauthausen as a guard. Something happened there that no one knows about, Hans said, but everyone in the village knew that the son of the Russian had volunteered for the front because of it. He was killed in battle at the place his father had come from, at Smolensk.

We had all fallen silent, though we were a little skeptical, about this fairy tale that Hans told us in such detail, about Hans himself, who stood before us like a force of nature, about his own cross to bear, and about his masquerade—we had all grown skeptical, yet we were rapt, the way people are when they are moved.

In the stable, a little deer was playing with a chick; the dog was running through the farm and chasing a rabbit. Later some geese showed up. We were sitting at a long table, and Hans was cooking; he used up all the eggs in his household and every bit of his strength to make the most delectable Kaiserschmarrn in the Reich. Then Hans composed verses to me, guessed my profession, complimented me by remarking that I notice everything. I rarely encounter men who are more intense than I. We talked about the war and laughed the whole time, maybe just because of the amusing animals and the invigorating air. We were surrounded by mountains, the reddish mountain pasture sank in the fog, Michael had plucked alpine roses for me, for the granddaughter of a prisoner of war, although it's prohibited, and I thought that all of us, even the Saudis at the head of the trail and the Orthodox Jews who had not come this year, were all part of a grand epic, a randomly illuminated part of it, a small stretch.

It's time to round up the cows, Hans said, and got into his jeep. We rode up toward the snow. From my experience in Ukraine, I was unaware that cows could be rounded up with a jeep; where I come from, a jeep and cows are worlds apart, and there lies an impassable swamp between them.

When we were back and I was already thinking about the milking and how I would be staying forever if I milked his cows, because milk erases your memory, I heard Hans announce, I have a nice little room for you, I won't disturb you, and although no one said anything, I sensed that they were in favor of this and were trying silently to persuade me to stay there, because my grandfather, the farmer, spent two years in captivity here, and now he was giving me the gift of the beauty of this world and all its freedoms. Here the laws of nature were at play that are sometimes so discernible that not only two people notice their effect, but everyone present, even those who have no connection to nature, and if I had the option of a sequel, I would stay here, just like the prisoner back then; I would volunteer and learn to milk, I thought, utterly unrealistically.

When Hans offered me a room for the night in earshot of the whole group, I said that he would have to drive me to Mauthausen in the morning with the jeep, and my inner voice said *Stop*.

Three times I had asked for the name of the dog who had chased the rabbits and the geese through the yard and then played with one of the geese; he had brought good cheer and comic relief into our group, so that we forgot all our woes. I've forgotten the dog's name. Two years later Hans ran over that dog and descended into a raw, impenetrable grief.

But back then I thought of the dog Tristan had given to Isolde, and how jaunty this creature of Hans's was. So many years had gone by since Tristan and Isolde met, yet they were only half as old as we are now. Tristan gave her a dog with a little bell to cheer her up and to help her forget him. Or was it the other way around, to remind her of him, but with joy? The name of that dog also slipped my mind, and I have also almost forgotten the misery that came over me as we left the robber Hans, because I had to go to Mauthausen, God knows why. A jeep ride didn't fit into my epic.

We left, and Hans waved goodbye.

Trip to Mauthausen

I get the feeling that all the passengers in the train—a strange combination of sports-minded people in shorts and hiking shoes, sleeping Japanese, and men in freshly pressed suits on their way to work in Salzburg, maybe even in Vienna—know where I'm heading and that I'm not one of them. I'm going there alone. I'm not part of the school classes that have to take this trip, I'm not one of those people who regard it as an educational journey, as a sure path to a greater awareness of history or as a kind of moral imperative. I'm alone on this trip, but I wish my fellow passengers could know—or if not, at least guess or sense—where I'm headed. As though it was so important and unusual to travel to Mauthausen. After all, some people do live there, in that modern baroque town, but I want them to know it, as though it would take their knowledge of my journey to lend it meaning, as though only then would I be in a position to declare my personal undertaking a pilgrimage. And although I am traveling to Mauthausen alone, I am doing it for the sake of all my fellow travelers without asking them. Yes, I will send regards from you, I'll see to it, dear people, you don't have to do it yourselves, forge ahead with your travels, but if you go hiking, please don't forget me, then we're even.

An elderly woman is amazed at me and my gear, at the network device to show me the way, at my iPhone with its functions I've yet to master, the headphones and the cables in various colors from various eras that I try in vain to connect up—this hodge-podge, this octopus, this web designed to set me in the right direction, ties up my hands and feet. Am I thinking about the milking equipment and of Hans's cows? I help the woman, somewhat faint with astonishment, carry her suitcase. She gets out in Salzburg, turns around to me, and says, in an unexpectedly stern voice, Have a grand tour! She had meant to say *Have a great trip*, but her slip of the tongue caught me in a moment of megalomania. In Linz, I ask for the bus to Mauthausen at the central bus station. Sure enough, it's bus number 360 to Mauthausen, a circle around the world.

I stand at the platform in the large bus station and wait. The number 360 confirms that I'm on the right path, that I'm moving in a circle. It would also prove that I'm still at the beginning of all journeys, but I continue calculating and subtract the 360 of the bus from the days of the year and think of the difference. Five, sometimes six days. Are these days the most important ones? Are they the days when something really happens, are they the only days that have meaning, and there cannot be any more than that in a year?

I photograph signs, timetables, and displays to prove I was here, not to others, but to myself. I don't ever do this; I have no pictures from even my most wonderful trips. I can't live and snap photos at the same time, but now I say to the moment, *Linger a while! Thou art so fair!* Snap. I'll understand later.

At first I was alone at the bus stop and speculated about whether buses could go there at all. I wasn't drawing any distinction between concentration camp, memorial site, and town. I thought the whole world saw that I was heading to Mauthausen, although there was no one around to see me. But then a group of young people with beach bags and inflatable swim rings arrived, clearly heading out on the 360 to go swimming, all of which I found acceptable, until a lady got in holding a toilet seat, also 360 degrees, a circle, though not a perfect one, of course; a life preserver would have been more appropriate. But let's not get upset with them, a thousand years have gone by since the war, which war was that? You can go to the bathroom, you can go climbing or swimming, and you can even have nice weather. A war that is long since over isn't incompatible with a bikini, take your mind off this lady, she's not a perpetrator or a victim, and now these words had to be said after all, she's smoking, making smoke rings, 360 degrees plus 5 days, only Marlene Dietrich could make such lovely smoke rings, maybe this lady plays chess as well, all she did was buy a toilet seat on this Wednesday.

The war is long since past, but you'd like to conscript the peaceful residents of the area around Linz with their swim rings and toilet seats, now, when it's so hot and they're going to swim? They were simply born here and live here. It's not their fault that this war is your origin, your history, your antiquity, and you're traveling from here to there and paying for it with only five to six days, this remainder of the circle, and if there hadn't been a war, you'd have no history and none of the causes that go along with it, as though you'd been born from Zeus's head, in full armor, but with a weak heel.

We rode through Linz. The Danube, sparkling from the sun, blinded me at every intersection. I was in a good mood, either because the houses were lovely or because I was determined to like the places we passed. Maybe I just wanted to be able to say that Linz is a beautiful city. Many young people were getting on and off, the kind of people who, when drafted, choose community service, conscientious objectors, my white guard. Or does everyone here work at memorial sites? A castle on the mountain, the Danube, a driver who enjoyed driving us there and told me that I ought to sit right up front with him, You can see better from here, ma'am, and he would show me where to get out, and I thought about how strange it is that people were annihilated in these cozy valleys—as though it was somehow acceptable in Siberia, where it's cold, barren, and flat.

My mind began to interlace two quotations I used to love back when I was young and loved quotations and thought people had three lives, fairy-tale style, as long as they armed themselves with literature: *Manuscripts don't burn* and *The letter always arrives at its destination*. These statements had made me hope that everything was just a matter of interpretation and nothing gets lost, but now they struck me as arrogant, cloying foolishness, mushy piety, maybe it was simply too hot here. I looked out the window and saw the yellowish fields, the soft hues and textures of the landscape. It would be better to take in these quotations separately, I was thinking, but now I've tossed them in together so as to leave them and their harsh aftertaste on these meadows and fields, manuscripts burn better than wood, and letters are constantly getting lost if they're written at all, and if they are, they're misunderstood, almost always, especially now the electronic ones.

I try to retrain my focus on the fabric of history, as I am traveling to Mauthausen, but it doesn't work, I think about clouds and meadows, stunning colorful dresses, and flowers, but history, the events; oh, I don't know, it's all fabric, fabric, and you can sew plenty with it, with velvet, satin, and crepe de chine. Or, as we said back in Russian, *krepdyshin*.

My babushka Rosa, who spent her whole life awaiting the return of her husband Vasya, Vasily, from all these camps that I am now visiting, had dresses of this kind. During the war she had saved two hundred children, and in her old age she looked like a child bloated with hunger. She was quite thin, but her belly was distended, and no dress fit her, so a seamstress made dresses for her, out of *krepdyshin* or silk. Bright green with white stripes, violet polka dots on the horizon of a sunny day, dark blue with white and black waves rolling through the landscape, and this fragrant, slightly shiny fabric with lilies and roses, a marvel in our homespun world. I would give half a kingdom and all the historical fabrics in the world to get my hands on a little piece of that silk. People will do anything to explain away death, as though there is no disappearance, only reception and arrival.

In one small town, passengers get in again, and everything is pretty, the market square and the people. Next stop is Gusen, the satellite camp of Mauthausen, which I've read about. We ride through quickly. The sharp gray wall of the memorial site is at an angle to the street, as though intent on slicing through the landscape. I continue to feel this slicing in my throat when the wall is long since behind us. A phantom pain, I can't swallow. Just before we get to Mauthausen, my nice bus driver catches a schoolgirl with an expired ID. He turns merciless, scathing; she glumly pays the usual four euros. Everyone concurs in silence; he's right. When I get out at the Wasserwerk station near Mauthausen, he's angry even at me. I've witnessed him getting cheated, he felt humiliated and hit back, and I saw that as well, a witness of the journey, and witnesses make it all worse.

My suitcase is stuck, and everyone is waiting, including the bus driver, and he isn't saying a word. I make frantic movements, but the suitcase won't budge. *I'm sorry!* He stays silent, stone-faced, self-righteous. I finally free my suitcase and set foot in Mauthausen. The sweat is pouring down my back.

Sisyphus

Sisyphus, who, according to the Greek myth, was condemned to roll a boulder up a steep mountain, only to have it roll back down, again and again, shortly before reaching the top, is spelled with an "i" in the first syllable, and with a "y" in the second. Also: Sisyphean task.

—DUDEN

On the hilltop I saw a fortress, reminiscent of the Middle Ages, whose massive walls, soaring towers, and impeccable, even flawless geometry struck me as beautiful, or at least pleasing. I had not thought that it would be beautiful here, I thought it couldn't possibly be appealing. The sight of it aroused my sense of dimension, proportion, and harmony, which was clearly the driving force for the creators of places like these.

visiting the memorial site as part of a longer bike tour. The small valley of the quarry, where the work took place, bears some resemblance to a national park somewhere in America, a rocky area with quite a bit of greenery, and a small waterfall set farther back; two bicycles are locked to a construction fence with a sign on top that says "Swimming is prohibited on the premises of the memorial site." Without passing judgment, Wolfgang describes the crimes of yesterday and the normality of today, a normality that assumes its place anew in every era. All that remains in my head is numbers.

Thirty nations were represented here, each has a monument. Politicians, workers, priests . . . I get a better picture of the European parliament here than I do in Brussels; anyone who was in a concentration camp can also enter the European Union. Five hundred Soviet officers attempted to escape; the whole region hunted them down in what came to be known as the *Hasenjagd* (hare hunt). The dead were brought together like slain game animals, not big beasts but cowardly little hares, but what does that mean, anyway, my notes say forty-seven thousand were cremated, a strange word wedged between the numbers, most of them died of malnutrition and disease, maybe it's wrong, I mean, maybe the number is wrong, as though numbers of this kind could ever be right, some hundred thousand people were murdered in Mauthausen or perished while performing hard labor. If a person was so many times bigger than an atom as the sun is bigger than a person, where would the midway point be between the death of an individual and the death of millions? Would it be a number, or the place where I'm now standing? I understand one, I understand ten, one hundred is hard, but one thousand? Often Jewish prisoners were thrown down into the quarry from an altitude of fifty meters; they were called "parachutists." One prisoner later reported that exactly one thousand Jewish prisoners were thrown from the cliff on the occasion of Heinrich Himmler's visit in the spring of 1941. An apple tree is on the premises, with enticing apples. The Kommandant is said to have given his son fourteen prisoners on his fourteenth birthday, hanged on an apple tree in the Kommandant's garden, arranged as tree ornaments. The fourteen yield more than the thousand, 14 > 1,000, more of what, more of something uncountable—is it the manner of their death, or is 14 a number that we can still make sense of, and beyond that, our mathematics break down? At what number does the individual disappear? Ten thousand people executed by shooting were buried under the Marbach linden, over there on the mountain, if I'm not mistaken, how am I supposed to imagine that, there were six hundred students in my school, and I've never been in a stadium. If I add on another zero, I have to begin thinking strategically; I'm picturing the big residential areas, in the high-rises on the island across from my house in Kiev there are exactly a hundred thousand residents. I surreptitiously introduce them into the death statistics without disturbing their sleep, not forever, just long enough to grasp this number, and then I bring them back to life.

We grew up with the statistic of twenty million war casualties; then it turned out that there were many more. We are indulged and spoiled by numbers, violated by presentations of violence; to understand these numbers is to accept the violence. A feeling of gloom washes over me; I don't know why all this sounds so ordinary, almost boring.

I wanted to find a solution, for myself and for those who live and work here today, I wanted to recall and record it, but it was an activity without a foreseeable end. Sisyphus sought to cheat death, and Thanatos punished him with never-ending labor, bringing him back to life from the realm of shadows and condemning him to eternal toil, eternal effort, eternal memory. Sisyphus rolled his boulder up, by the sweat of his brow, and we know how that turned out.

Care was taken to keep the rooms and walkways in the camp clean, flower boxes mounted on the barracks and the sandy paths smoothed with a road roller, because the world is beautiful, only the prisoners were filthy and ailing, unworthy of living, created solely for the work that would destroy them, again and again they carried boulders to the top, following one another step by step, many abreast, like a crowd scene in a movie, anyone who stumbled dragged down others, dozens fell like dominoes, injured or dead, and if one was stronger than this work, he could still be shot to death. There were also poets here, maybe they had tried to cheat death and were now being punished.

I saw the top of the hill, felt the weight, thought about the danger, and started to roll my boulder upward, but my stories hadn't grasped the nature of the place. I could not recount a thing, not even that here a human being was allowed only to fail. It did not add up and it made no sense. Why not leave the boulder in place?

When we left, the memorial site was already closed, and an aging man in a white undershirt came running toward us, once again and spoke to everyone he met, farmers, priests, people who had been children at the time . . . He describes churches, winding streets, and cemeteries. He tells the stories of farmers watching dying people walk by and being forbidden to help them—even looking at them was forbidden. Potatoes were being planted at this time, and the farmers secretly threw food onto the path or stuck it into the fences; one woman reports that the Jews were keen for onions, *I couldn't put them into their hands, I threw the onions to them, but one of the guards told me that he could shoot me as well*, one girl denounced Jews who had hidden at the cemetery, and another girl was amazed that those who could no longer walk were not only shot to death, but also beaten up in this lovely area, a man who had to gather up the corpses with his cart remembered the numbers, and there were women and children, and other women and children who stood by and watched, and one woman recalled that there were no more leaves on the trees once they had gone by, and I also remember plums, I even remember a young German guard who plucked plums for the Jews, but it was in April, you have to know that, there were neither plums nor good deeds, a little boy tried to carry his collapsing father, but often the end of these stories is missing, the farmers didn't hear all the shots, and I read and read until they had arrived exactly where my grandfather had been, in Gunskirchen. I tried to imagine how he observed the arrivals and what happened next, but I wasn't able to, and then I read the translations from Hungarian, *We got a good place anyway, Uncle Geza fought to get it*, until I reached the point that I couldn't go on, my emotional repository was full with the dead in the woods, and I started to make copies of the loose sheets of paper, because, as we all know, machines are made for eliminating our incapabilities, or should I say ex-

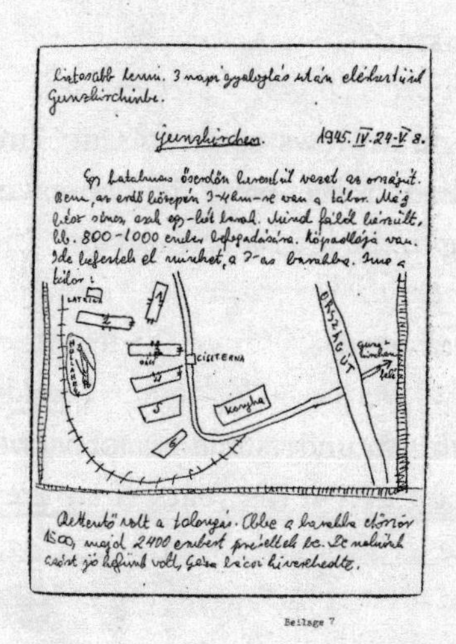

Biztosabb lenni. 3 napi gyaloglás után elérkeztünk Gunskirchenbe.

Gunskirchen. 1945. IV. 24 - V. 8.

Egy hatalmas őserdőn keresztül vezet az országút. Benn, az erdő közepén 3-4 km-re van a tábor. Még kész sincs, csak egy-két barak. Mind fából készült, kb. 800-1000 ember befogadására. Kőpadlója van. Ide fektettek el minket, a 7-es barakkba. Íme a tábor:

Rettentő volt a tolongás. Ebbe a barakkba először 1500, majd 2400 embert préseltek be. De nekünk csak jó helyünk volt, Géza bácsi kiverekedte.

Beilage 7

panding our capabilities, and I was making copies as though I could have extended or even duplicated someone's life in the act of copying,

I wasn't even looking at the pages, there were pictures on them that were not meant for me, I caught only a glimpse of them and was sure that I would never look at them again, *but I need them!* and pressed the button, thus producing more pounds of atrocities, however, in this process of duplication something happened that we need machines for, and I pressed the button as though this machine could serve to salvage something, I made copies of everything and felt my own future growing and expanding as I continued to make copies of Gunskirchen and in the process putting off more and more the contemplation of what it all meant, which I might not get to experience at all, and I kept making copies until I began to realize that as usual I was drawing no distinction between the e in the German word *gerettet* (saved) and the similar-sounding ä in *Geräte* (machines), and was unwittingly seeking salvation from this machine.

What I was thinking—

when the Hungarian Jews came to Gunskirchen, was my grandfather already there, were the non-Jewish men forced to do something to the Jewish prisoners?

that the worst survived

I am doing all this to understand his forty-two days in Gunskirchen and the thirty-seven years of his life back home, if only for one line

I want to go home

he was exactly the age I am now

I have lost sight of him yet again

if the world is like this, there is no point in living, this idea does not imply weakness

a child on its mother's lap

that there was barely any water in the camp, and if my grandfather survived it means that someone had to die in his place, but I've already said that

of the word *KZler*, meaning concentration camp prisoner, in the documents, one *KZler*, eight *KZlers*, *KZlers* here, there, and everywhere

---

two elderly American men meeting somewhere in the middle of the United States, maybe in Texas, and talking about Gunskirchen, about how their unit had stumbled upon thousands of starving people in the woods, and how thousands died in the days that followed after getting food from the men who'd rescued them

how an Israeli family traveled to Gunskirchen after finding the diary of the deceased father who had survived Mauthausen, Gusen, and Gunskirchen, a seventeen-year-old from Budapest who survived because he made an obsessive habit of counting everything, the steps, the trees, the people, the stripes. He said nothing to his children, and now these four adult siblings were in the woods outside Gunskirchen, looking for the father they no longer knew. One of them made a film about it called *Six Million and One*, as though this calculation had made individual people out of a monolithic number, *six million* turning into *six million ones*

that you see or do something, and it is then forever

I don't know where this conviction stemmed from, but it was right here in this small camp that something happened after everything that had happened already that made my grandfather's return home impossible, so that he, back in Kiev, could not stay with his family, not with his daughters and not with his wife, Rosa, whose mother and sister lie in Babi Yar, which makes a person Jewish forever, I know that his failure to return had something to do with the death march of the Hungarian Jews

———

maybe my grandfather saw someone in this crowd of women and children who resembled his own family

that certainty lies in conjecture

Benno, the seventeen-year-old brother of my newfound relative, Mira Kimmelman, number 133856 from Mauthausen, was shot to death in March 1945 on one of the numerous marches from Mauthausen to somewhere; he couldn't go on, as an eyewitness said

that relatives meet up on paths like this, and that here all are related

of the death march on Google Maps

Ivan Myatchin, I've yet to mention him, another seventeen-year-old. He was the only one my grandfather spoke about. Ivan worked in the camp's kitchen, and when he found out that Vasily had two daughters, he tried to get him leftovers, because Ivan believed that it would be better for Vasily to survive than for the boys with no children. Vasya survived, and thought it was on account of Ivan, but maybe he just wanted to be grateful to someone for his survival, otherwise he'd be left with nothing but guilt, but we don't know in which camp they met, there's no Ivan Myatchin on the Mauthausen lists.

in the Soviet Union there were ten million more women than men after the war—or twenty

---

my grandfather Vasily came home, but for a brief time only. Everyone had been waiting for him, and my grandmother, Rosa, had saved his favorite leather coat throughout the war in spite of the evacuation and the death of close relatives. Vasily was there again, and they fought, maybe not constantly, but often. First the coat disappeared, and then Vasily went as well.

The End of the Empire

I'm convinced that my trip through Austria was staged—but by whom? I was following the traces of captivity in the war; I met Saudis, the giant Hans, and two presidents who had landed on the lawn in front of Mauthausen with their helicopters, like a scene from *Apocalypse Now*, accompanied by the "Ride of the Valkyries," and in the cities doors were held open for me by men I didn't know. When I finally arrived in Vienna, where the war archives were housed, and where Ozjel, the father of my grandmother Rosa, was born, Otto von Habsburg had just died, and the newspapers were writing about the end of the old Europe, about seven hundred years of the Habsburgs, a dynasty that had shaped the history of several centuries, they were writing about World War I and what would have become of the century, now well behind us, if Otto von Habsburg had become kaiser or at least an influential figure in European politics, and the newspapers also said that this was truly the end. Not a word about how this dynasty led Europe into World War I. The city was adorned for the lavish funeral; people walked more slowly than our time allowed for. I, too, walked slowly and solemnly along the wide and narrow streets of Vienna, like dancers in the last act, a pair, when they make their way past the ranks of their subjects hand in hand and triumphantly arrive at the end of the performance. I walked alone and saw black ribbons being hung out of the windows along the path of the funeral procession, and thought of a different procession; in my mind I was still with my never-ending column.

La-La-La Human Step was the name of the dance performance where I met another Hans. We went dancing afterward. Hans was a DJ from Germany; he told me about Dionysus, his cult and his women, about the loss of self-consciousness that comes with rhythm, about abandonment and trance, masses in movement in our globalized world. Hundreds of people were dancing with us, and at some point we talked about our grandfathers who were prisoners of war, his as a German in Siberia, mine as a Russian in Austria, we raved, or we were raving for peace, the whole night, for world peace, for Dionysus and in memory of Otto von Habsburg. When I left the next day, I rode through Vienna one last time, past barriers, police, coaches, cavalrymen and military brass; there were elderly people on the street as well, in colorful clothing and festooned hats, looking as though they'd been resurrected from one of those 1950s films about Sissi the Austrian Empress, subjects of their own past, but I missed out on Otto von Habsburg's funeral as well as the promised end of Europe.

meaningless dull light about. / You may live another quarter century; / All will still be there. No way out. / You die. You start again and all / Will be repeated as before: / The cold rippling of a canal. / The night. The street. Street-lamp. Drugstore." It's a mystery to me why we never asked who this dear servant was, and why we didn't understand that even the numerous princes with their white horses and castles had stolen into our childhood from the German fairy tales.

When I went back to the intersection of Institutskaya and Liebknecht, in the direction of the streetlight, drugstore, and the house in which Ozjel died and I was born, I thought about my mother telling me how our house still had black numbers on the doors for many years after the war; German military headquarters was located there during the occupation, but the neighbors said no, it was the Ukrainian police, and no matter how much people tried, they could not get rid of the black paint. Although no one from that time was still living there, not even from my time, and there were now air conditioners and glassed-in balconies, I was drawn to this place. When I stood facing the house I could call my own, and wondered whether we had lived on the second or the third floor at the time I was born, an old lady came out of the drugstore. She smiled, and I smiled back. She was dressed in white, with a long white coat and white shoes; even her hair was white, and it shone in a faint white light on this foggy day. We stood side by side at the intersection for one long minute, our traffic lights displayed the seconds, after thirty seconds she was still smiling, she was looking over at me in seeming recognition and in certainty I would never recognize her, and then she said—or was she chiding me?—I've been meeting you here somewhat too often lately! And I replied in amazement that I hadn't been there for years. That doesn't matter, she said.

The light turned green. I was so astonished that I stood there and did not notice the lady disappearing from view. When I looked around, it was red again, and she was gone, vanished into thin air, and I thought, she's right, I do come back here too often, yes of course, I thought, somewhat too often.

ACKNOWLEDGMENTS

I would like to thank my parents, Miron Petrowskij and Svetlana Petrowskaja, for having faith in me—and for surprising me with their appreciation of a book that I wrote for them and about them, in a language they don't know.

My greatest thanks go to my husband, Tobias Münchmeyer. He was the first one my father entrusted with the story of Maybe Esther. He is the force behind this book and the person I'm addressing in it. He was at my side from the outset, and I thank him for his devoted and tireless help in finding words, developing ideas, and getting us through our everyday tasks.

Sieglinde Geisel accompanied me on my quest for the right expressions throughout the writing process. She threw herself into this project, and the book would not have been possible without her patience, her enthusiasm, and our bond of friendship.

My editor, Katharina Raabe, reinforced my resolve to write the book, and supported me during all phases of my writing with her attentive trust.

I would like to thank everyone who helped with my research. Their generosity often went far beyond the call of duty: Halina Hila Marcinkowska and Anna Gawrzyjał (Kalisz), Anna Przybyszewska Drozd, Yale J. Reisner and Jan Jagielski (the Emanuel Ringelblum Jewish Historical Institute,

Warsaw), my dear brother Yohanan Petrovsky-Shtern (Northwestern University), Annemarie Zierlinger (St. Johann), Michael Mooslechner (Flachau), Wolfgang Schmutz (Mauthausen Memorial), Mira Kimmelman and her family (Oak Ridge and Washington), and Rosalyn and Eshagh Shaoul, who proved that family is much bigger than you might think. Kornel Miglus, Maciej Gutkowski, Grzegorz Kujawa, Michael Abramovich, Yevgenia Belorusets.

Thank you to all my teachers and friends.

Thanks also go to the Robert Bosch Foundation for its support in the framework of the Border Crossers program, and to the Künstlerhaus Lukas (and the state of Mecklenburg-Vorpommern), for the fellowship to conduct my work.

ILLUSTRATION CREDITS

PAGE 25: Lida Sinyakova, ca. 1957. Family archive.

PAGE 54: Rosalia Krzewina, ca. 1991. Family archive.

PAGE 83: Ozjel Krzewin and his pupil.

PAGE 84: Krzewin's school for the deaf and mute, Kiev, 1916. Family archive.

PAGE 85: Abram Silberstein.

PAGE 96: Graffiti in Warsaw, 2012. Photo: K. P.

PAGE 113: Embroiderers, 1925. From *Seifer Kalisz* (Tel Aviv, 1968).

PAGE 119: Cobblestones, Kalisz, 2012. Photo: K. P.

PAGE 132: Nikolaus Basseches, "Trial of Dead Souls," April 18, 1932. Archive of the Berlin Foreign Office.

PAGE 139 and 157: Judas Stern. From *Vossische Zeitung*, April 17, 1932.

PAGE 143: Trial of Sergey Vasilyev and Judas Stern. From *Vossische Zeitung*, April 17, 1932.

PAGE 197: Corner of Luteranskaya and Meringovskaya Streets, November 25, 1941. From D. Malakov, *Kiew, 1941–1943: Fotoalbum* (Kiev 2000).

PAGE 243: Report of an inmate at Gunskirchen. Archive of the Mauthausen Memorial, Federal Ministry for the Interior, Vienna.

ABOUT THE TRANSLATOR

SHELLEY FRISCH's numerous translations from the German, which include biographies of Friedrich Nietzsche, Albert Einstein, Leonardo da Vinci, Marlene Dietrich, Leni Riefenstahl, and Franz Kafka, have been awarded Modern Language Association and Helen and Kurt Wolff translation prizes. She lives in Princeton, New Jersey.